LETTERS FROM AL

from NATIONAL REVIEW

Andrews and McMeel
A Universal Press Syndicate Company
Kansas City

D1711456

Designed by Barrie Maguire

Library of Congress Cataloging-in-Publication Data

Letters from Al : from national review.
    p.   cm.
    ISBN : 0-8362-1754-3
    1. Gore, Albert, 1948- –Humor. United States–Politics and government–1993- –Humor. I. National review.
E840.8.G65L48   1994
973.929'092–dc20   94-7026
                                        CIP

INTRODUCTION

When Bill Clinton won the presidency, my colleagues at *National Review* and I realized at once that a great opportunity beckoned. Well before the fountains of Whitewater began gushing rumors of land deals and insider trading, it was plain that the new administration—directed and staffed equally by Good Ol' Boys, Stern Unbending Feminists, and Teenagers—would be a wonderful place to visit. What would happen when the chicanery hit the politics of virtue? We needed a source right at the heart of things to keep our readers fully informed.

Vice President Albert Gore, Jr., fit the bill perfectly. He is a mere heartbeat away from the President, thus closer even than the First Lady. He is upright, sober, solemn, and humorless in precisely the way that makes someone funny to other people. And being both honest and guileless, he would be an ideal reporter, telling us more than he himself realized about the shenanigans going on around him.

If Mr. Gore did not exist, it would be necessary to invent him. Since he does exist but is unlikely to contribute regularly to *National Review,* we invented him anyway as "Al," the Vice President in his private capacity. Our principal model was the Vice President's public personality, if that is not an exaggeration. But "Al" also harks back to Mr. Pooter, the immortal protagonist of George and Weedon Grossmith's *Diary of a Nobody,* a Victorian London clerk with ideas above his station, who solemnly records the tricks played by his friends and the offenses to his dignity, without ever realizing that he is a figure of fun fallen among thieves.

How would Vice President Pooter tell us about the White House follies? A diary? Letters? Memoranda to his aides? An early draft of his memoirs? There are satirical precedents for all of these. The British magazine, *Private Eye,* used to publish accounts of life in Mrs. Thatcher's Downing Street by "Dennis Thatcher" in letters to his golfing pal, "Bill." It currently runs "The Secret Diary of John Major, Age 47¾." In the end we thought that the epistolary form would work best. Hence, letters to his environmentalist pen pal, "Rusty," camped out in the Brazilian rain forest to prevent it from catching fire.

No politician writes his own speeches these days, and Vice President Pooter had, of course, the assistance of a ghost in composing this correspondence. This particular ghost wishes to remain in the shadows. He thinks that ghosts should know that their place is not in the Style Page. Besides, he does not wish to detract from the real contribution of Vice President Gore whose public appearances have generously confirmed that this is truly the inside dope.

JOHN O'SULLIVAN
EDITOR, *NATIONAL REVIEW*

THE VICE PRESIDENT
WASHINGTON

Dear Rusty:

Well, here I am. My first official act as Vice President is to write my cherished friend Rusty a long overdue letter. I thought of you often while on the campaign trail, and once or twice during campaign stops, time permitting, I shared with the crowd some of the experiences I had while visiting you and the other researchers down in Brazil. And boy, when I got to those relative-deforestation-vs-replanting-to-avoid-topsoil-erosion-figures, let me tell you, that cheering, screaming crowd of well-wishers got pretty darn quiet and reflective.

Do you remember that night during my last visit, as we sat along the banks of the Rio Kuluene and I told you that my secret goal was to live aboard a space station high above the Earth, trying to heal the ozone layer from the outside? Do you remember what you said to me? You looked me in the eye and you said, "Senator" (I was still Senator then!), "I think you'll probably have more effect if you stayed here on the Earth." And then you told me that I was sitting in a patch of grass the Yanonami Indians call "the grass of a thousand burning needles."

Well, you were right. I can have more effect here on the Earth, especially in my capacity as Vice President. But let me be very honest and tell you, strictly between us, that I'm a little worried about the future of Bill's and my Administration. First we had a problem with getting an attorney general. The first nominee had hired a couple from Peru illegally. Boy, did that turn into a big deal. The first thing I did was call Dad and ask about the status of Consuela and Esperanza, and he assured me that they were "as legal as two people from Mexico can be," which put my mind at ease.

-2-

So there we were in the Oval Office—me, Bill, Warren Christopher, Lloyd Cutler with a big binder of women's names, and Hillary on the speakerphone (she was driving back from a meeting with Les Aspin and Colin Powell) and I kept thinking, "This is it, this is the first big test." As we flipped through Lloyd's scrapbook rejecting people, the perfect candidate occurred to me: Tipper! The minute I mentioned it, the meeting came to a halt. Hillary started coughing or something, and Bill stared thoughtfully ahead, biting his bottom lip as he does. Then Hillary said that she was planning to offer Tipper a spot on her health-care crisis team, so I backed down. But for a minute there, Rusty, Tipper and I almost became Washington's Power Couple!

The crisis resolved itself satisfactorily. We nominated a terrific prosecutor from Miami, who—are you sitting down?— lives out on the Everglades, part of America's Endangered Wetlands! I think I've sent a message to the press with this one: I am a Vice President with influence.

At first I was a little worried about my influence in the Administration. Inauguration Day, one of the Marines introduced Bill and Hillary as "the President of the United States, William Jefferson Clinton, and the Vice President . . ." and then he caught himself, and quickly said, ". . . and the First Lady, Hillary Clinton." She nudged him angrily, and to tell you the truth, I felt sorry for the guy. It was just a simple slip-up. But she whispered something in his ear, and he piped up again: ". . . and the First Lady, Hillary Rodham Clinton." I thought the whole thing was pretty funny, but I was up till three in the morning trying to show Tipper the humor of it all. She can be a little paranoid. We had a few blow-ups along the campaign trial. When Bill offered to show our girls how to play a few essential chords on the saxophone, Tipper pulled Stephanopoulous aside and demanded a separate campaign bus.

During the budget-deficit crisis, I've tried to serve as a quiet, disinterested counselor to Bill, a sounding board, if you will.

One Sunday afternoon, we were all up at Camp David working on the economic plan; I knew Bill was feeling low. Stan Greenberg, his pollster, had come in with the news that no President had ever had a lower approval rating at this point in his Administration. The talk shows had been filled with discussions of his mistakes—nothing about our accomplishments, of course—and he clearly needed a boost. "Bill," I said, "let's you and me go for a run and clear our heads. What about it?" Just as he was about to put on his jogging shoes, Hillary walked in with about a dozen pizzas and said, "I thought if we work through dinner, we could finish trimming 30 percent from the NASA budget." Bill sat down in front of a spreadsheet and a pizza and went to work.

I stuck around for the rest of the session. Hillary kept wanting to cut funding for the space station, I had given my word to some former colleagues on the Hill that it was untouchable. So we went back and forth about it until finally she turned to me and said, "If we fund it and build it, will you go live in it?"

How did she know?

Take care, Rusty. Give Ya'nammeole a hug for me.

THE VICE PRESIDENT

WASHINGTON

Dear Rusty:

Well, Bill and Hillary and I came up with a plan to fix the economy! Are you happy or what? I'm sure you don't get much timely news down there in the rain forest, but let me be very honest with you: it's a huge success. All across the country, people are excited about paying more in taxes.

But to be totally frank with you, I feel a little let down. You know, back in '88 when I was running for President, if you mentioned raising taxes you could kiss the election good-bye. Now, the people are actually happy to be paying more taxes. They can't seem to get enough. Boy, is Bill a lucky guy! When I ran, the country was still in its selfish phase. Okay, I know this is going to sound like sour grapes, but deep down, I know I could have raised taxes more than he can. Frankly, strictly between us, my level of commitment is higher.

Bill pretty much sequestered himself in the Oval Office during the days leading up to our speech. Hillary came and explained to me that Bill needed some "alone time," which I respected. No one got to see him, and I mean no one, except for Hillary, Mack McLarty, Colin Powell, Ron Brown, George Stephanopoulos, Lloyd Bentsen, Linda Bloodworth-Thomason, Leon Panetta, Bruce Babbitt, Donna Shalala, and Marian Wright Edelman. Oh, I suppose a few others might have slipped in too.

From the outside, it might look like I was being shut out. Tipper certainly read it that way. She kept after me to be more assertive. I tried to reason with her. I told her that I was going to be Vice President for four years, that my influence had to grow and develop over time, that as men grow close to each other, like Bill and I have, we need time to heal the wounds we each carry from our fathers before we can truly bond.

Tipper wouldn't hear a word of it. Remember that time I casually mentioned that maybe we should pull Al Jr. and the

-2-

girls out of school and all go live by the Orinoco River in
Brazil? Remember her reaction? Well, the days before the
budget speech were close to that. She kept telling me to barge
into the office, to make my presence known. We argued and
argued.

One night I was working late in my office, all alone, on the
Timber Summit (an idea that Hillary and I cooked up to bring
attention to the timber problems in the Pacific Northwest. It
was her idea, actually. "This ought to keep you busy," she said.
And boy, has it ever!) and I was hunched over my desk, lost in
thought, when two hands suddenly covered my eyes. "Guess
who!" I heard. It was Tipper. She had come to make up. She
told me she was sorry for pushing me. She wanted to have a
romantic "picnic" in my office. She held up two big bags from
McDonald's and a bucket of fried chicken. Normally I don't eat
that kind of food, but the gesture was so sweet I didn't say
anything. She also brought two pizzas, ribs and biscuits, and
several meatball subs. The whole West Wing smelled like a
junk-food restaurant. I said, "Is all this food for us?" and she
said, "I just want you to know how much I love you." She's
such a special lady.

I had just picked up a slice of pizza when Bill appeared at
the door! He must have smelled the food all the way in the
Oval Office. He looked tired and worn out. I guess he had been
getting by without much sleep. We made some small talk, and
the whole time he didn't take his eyes off the food. Tipper got
that little smile she gets when she's embarrassed and said,
"Well, I guess you two probably have a lot to talk about,"
and she left. So there I was, eating pizza and ribs with Bill
at one in the morning, just the two of us, like we were still
campaigning. We talked about the budget speech, the economic
plan, health care, topsoil erosion—all the big issues.
Just him and me.

I got home very late that night and I felt great. Tipper and I
had made up; Bill and I had gotten even closer—and we were
pretty close before. I crawled into bed, thanked Tipper for the
picnic, and apologized for the interruption. "Don't worry," she
said. "The only way to get face time with that man is when
he's stuffing his." I was too tired to argue.

Letters from Al

-3-

After the big speech, Bill and I flew all across the country selling our program of taxes, fees, and job programs. The response was overwhelming. People are really ready for big government again. As Bill and I walked across the tarmac to board Air Force One, Tipper called after me, ran up, gave me a big kiss, and slipped about a dozen Snickers bars into my pockets. I told her that I never eat candy, but all she said was "I just want to show you how much I love you." Everyone saw it, even Bill, and I got embarrassed. As we boarded the plane, Bill just couldn't take his eyes off my bulging pockets. Finally, I offered him a Snickers. As he ate it, he said, "Al, stick close today, okay? I'm going to need you next to me."

As we taxied down the runway, I looked out the window to see Tipper waving good-bye, smiling her wide, beautiful smile.

Hope all is well with you, Rusty. Save a date in August for the Timber Summit!

THE VICE PRESIDENT
WASHINGTON

March 22, 1993

Dear Rusty:

Things are getting rough! Our budget package is up for a vote, and we are lobbying like mad to get it passed. I'm not sure why—we've got the votes. Still, somebody in the White House is playing hardball.

I mentioned this to HRC, and she kind of squinched up her face the way she does when Bill and I hug. She and Susan Thomases had just come back from AV, an Italian restaurant on New York Avenue, and Thomases had a take-out bag. I mentioned I had received a call from Senator Shelby of Alabama. He couldn't vote for the package, and asked if I'd intercede with HRC for him. So I suggested we should be more flexible, since we've got the votes we need. HRC unsquinched her face and sighed. I got a little nervous because Thomases was there. She scares me.

Remember that time we were paddling up the Kuelene Tributary, and I got bitten by that little black bug that will soon be extinct if we don't pass a biodiversity law, and you told me not to scratch but I scratched anyway, and my forearm got really, really big and kind of green? And do you remember that you took me to see Ha'jakeleole, the Yanonami medicine woman, and what her face looked like as she sucked the poison out of my arm? Well, that's the way Susan Thomases looks at me all the time.

HRC told me that Shelby's going to get just what he deserves, and she and Thomases kind of half laughed, half grunted. Then as she walked by, Thomases tossed her take-out bag at me and said, "Here, mountain man. Recycle this." So at least she's reaching out.

I was still worried about Shelby when I heard on CNN that Dick Armey had made an impertinent remark, something about Bill being a one-termer like Jimmy Carter, which I took as a personal insult since that makes me Walter Mondale. Armey's obsessed with taxes and government spending and economic growth—a real troublemaker. But I have to be honest and say that I was a little worried about what might hit him. Ordinarily, I wouldn't care what she would do to a Republican, but I think Armey's conservative economic theories are byproducts of his wounded inner child. If I could have a weekend with Armey—just him and me—I know he'd see the light.

Since I was scheduled to visit Texas, I dropped by the Oval Office to confer. A secretary handed me two pieces of paper to take to the President. The first was a phone message from Dick Armey. He probably wants to make up, I thought. The second was a budget directive, asking Bill to delay transferring one hundred Space Shuttle jobs to Texas. I made a mental note to give them to Bill before our meeting ended.

When I walked in, Bill just lit up. That's the kind of friendship we've developed in six months. Close.

"You smell like Italian food," Bill said. I told him what happened with Thomases and the bag from AV and how I think she's warming up to me, and he smiled that smile he gets when he talks to little kids. Then he got serious. "So you don't have any food on you?" he asked. "I've got a box of Tic Tacs," I said. He thought for a minute, then said, "Gimme."

Just then, HRC walked in. Bill swallowed the Tic Tacs in a hurry, and kind of coughed. I offered to excuse myself, but Bill quickly said that wasn't necessary. HRC, though, thought it was. I thanked her for her honesty and left. The Secret Service agent in the hall looked upset. "Is she in there alone with him?" he asked. I nodded. He went pale. He pulled out the radio mike in his lapel and shouted into it, "Alice is in with Ralph! Alice is in with Ralph! Repeat: The Kramdens are alone together!" Everyone in the outer office cleared out. I was left standing there.

"They fight, sir," explained the Secret Service agent, "a lot." I wasn't satisfied. "Every couple fights, Agent Williams. Now get up off the floor and maintain your post." I learned to talk this way as an Army journalist in Vietnam. I don't like to do it because it brings up a lot of unresolved feelings I have about

-3-

my father, but sometimes the situation calls for it.

We heard a crash from the Oval Office. Then shouting, and then the sound of a piece of Jefferson china smashing into the wall. Bill was shouting, "But Hill, we have to delay the health-care-reform package; I can't raise taxes twice in one year, you moron! What do you think I am?" And she yelled back, "A coward! That's what." Crash. Bang. Pretty soon, I was down with my hands over my head like Agent Williams.

"The funny thing is, sir," he whispered to me, "what she's doing constitutes felonious behavior. She's physically attacking the President of the United States. Technically, I could go in there and shoot her."

He had just spoken, when the alarm bells rang. Bill had pushed the secret distress button beneath the top drawer of his desk. Williams just lay there. "Aren't you supposed to do something, Agent Williams?" I asked. He shook his head. "He pushes that button a lot when they're together. We're learning to adapt."

After my Texas trip, I read in the Post that the budget hardball continued. Dick Armey was being punished by not getting his phone calls returned, and poor Senator Shelby had to explain to constituents why a lot of Space Shuttle jobs had been transferred to Texas. HRC can be too vindictive, if you ask me.

Write soon, Al

THE VICE PRESIDENT
WASHINGTON

April 1, 1993

Dear Rusty:

Talk about an exciting two weeks! The budget package sailed through. Yeltsin was nearly ousted. I chaired the first meeting of the Health Care Task Force. The Timber Summit is finally becoming a reality. I've been on a "high" for ten days. I've been trying to contain my excitement in public, but you know me: my face always gives me away.

Things started out terrifically last Monday, and then they kept getting better. I let HRC know the Timber Summit was arranged, set, and fully planned. Boy, did she look shocked. "Already?" she asked. "I thought it would take you longer. At least until after the Health Care Reform Act."

"No, no," I told her. "It's all set." To be totally honest, Rusty, I liked catching her off guard. But I also felt pretty guilty. I mean, here I was getting all the glory, impressing the heck out of HRC, and the truth is, Tipper took over the whole project last month.

We were out to dinner with Bill and HRC—just the four of us, at one of our favorite South American places. You ate there once with us, do you remember? It was a few days after we first met in my Senate office, when you came by to lobby for increased rain-forest research money. At dinner, I asked you if I could do some research on the Orinoco with you. Tipper turned red, came down with that horrendous coughing fit, and I had to drive her home.

Well, it was in that very booth that we sat with Bill and HRC. The four of us had a great time. It was like being on the campaign all over again. Me and Bill making jokes, clapping each other on the back, and HRC and Tipper studying the menus quietly.

Of course, by the time the salads arrived, the Timber Summit had come up. I had about ten napkins covered with graphs, diagrams, maps, and sketches, and I was explaining to Bill the different ways the timber industry can be regulated so that only 37,000 jobs are lost (but not to Mexico), and he had that heavy-lidded look he gets when he's concentrating really hard. Tipper and HRC were quietly reading the No Smoking sign when HRC turned to Tipper and said, "Al's working so hard on that Timber Summit. I'm sure he'll be relieved when we go to Vancouver to meet Yeltsin. That'll give him a few days here, alone, without interruptions." Tipper kind of coughed, but she quickly swallowed some water and was okay.

As soon as the first course arrived, I put away the napkins, and the conversation kind of stopped while Bill ate. But as soon as they had cleared the dessert plates, we picked right up again, just talking and laughing like the very close friends we are. I pointed out that the restaurant has a booth way in the back, behind a couple of plants, totally out of view. Bill seemed pretty interested in it. Tipper and I celebrated our most recent wedding anniversary in that back booth. I nudged Bill. "That's where you can have a very private, very romantic dinner." Just then HRC was overcome with a pretty major coughing fit, and we left. You know what I think? I think it's the paella.

At home, I was getting into my pajamas when Tipper asked me, out of the blue, "Al, where's that Timber Summit supposed to take place?" "In the Northwest," I told her. "Near Vancouver?" she asked. "Pretty close," I replied.

She looked away for a moment, lost in thought. Then she looked at me steadily. "Al," she said, "I'm going to organize that Timber Summit for you."

And she did! What a woman!

So there I was, claiming credit for the Timber Summit, and feeling—can I be honest?—feeling terrific. I'm getting jaded, Rusty. They call it "Potomac fever." Maybe it's time I spent a few weeks with you in the rain forest, sleeping in that tent with the big hole in the top so that you can gaze at the stars through all the mosquitoes. What did you call it? Oh yeah—"the senator's tent." Boy, we had some good times together. I really miss you, Rusty. Next to Bill, you're one of my closest friends.

Tipper set the date for the Timber Summit for the day before Bill and HRC meet with Yeltsin. At first I was against it,

-3-

because I didn't think that we should be holding two such important events so close together. No need to steal our own thunder. But then Tipper explained that Bill and I could go in the same plane, thus saving a lot—I mean, a lot—of fuel, and well, I mean that just makes so much sense. And I could just tag along with Bill and HRC and the three of us could meet with Yeltsin.

Everybody was thrilled with that plan except HRC, who had a hard time believing the Summit (Timber, not Yeltsin) had been organized so quickly. I could tell she was a little suspicious when she turned to me at a meeting and said, "So did your wife do this?" I think she's worried that I won't have enough to do.

She had a brainstorm. She put me in charge of the very high-profile National Performance Review Board. Our job is to review every single government agency, program, bureau, and department, to ferret out waste and abuse, and to remodel each for efficiency and productivity. It's a terrific challenge, and I'll get a lot of good publicity. HRC has been very generous. She's even given me a six-month deadline. That's enough time, don't you think?

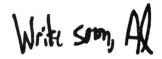

Write soon, Al

THE VICE PRESIDENT
WASHINGTON

April 19, 1993

Dear Rusty,

As hard as it is to believe, my first 100 days are almost up! To be totally honest, my report card has got to be pretty much like the ones I got at St. Alban's and Harvard—straight A's! But I've got to tell you, it's a lot like that Grateful Dead song that Tipper and I enjoy so much: it's been a very eventful journey.

The Summit was one of the most emotional and moving moments of my life. Two ancient enemies, brought together at the table—the environmentalists and the timber industry—while Bill and I facilitated an exchange of views. To be honest, Rusty, when it was time to go and we all shook hands, I got a little choked up. You know how emotional I get.

From there to Vancouver—another summit of sorts, between Yeltsin and Bill and me. Not much to report.

Back home, I got busy on my new challenge: the National Performance Review Board. This is an HRC brainstorm where I get six months to overhaul the entire Federal Government. Everything but the National Health Care System, which HRC says should be up and running by December. That and Defense. And farm subsidies.

But everything else is fair game. And boy, am I going at it. HRC helped out by suggesting at a press conference that we have an "800" number—kind of an electronic suggestion box. But the minute she gave out the number, the calls came in so fast that they overloaded the system. Boy, did I have egg on my face.

But to be truthful, it wasn't our fault. The outdated Bush-Reagan phone system can only handle a couple of thousand calls at one time. Bill and I have often discussed updating the technology at the White House. Did you know that when we arrived, we discovered the Bush Administration had been using computers almost eight years old?! Talk about archaic. And

-2-

don't quote me on this, but I think using that outdated equipment really hindered the past two Presidents. I joked to Bill that our Administration is going to need i486DX processors just to keep up with all our new regulations. And when we have that technology superhighway in place, we can beam new laws and regulations instantly across the country, more efficiently than ever before. It's a brave new world, Rusty. Especially for the public sector.

My first act for the National Performance Review Board, or "Al's Board," as HRC calls it, was to convene an electronic video meeting of Department of Agriculture workers. Did I get an earful!

You can't imagine how many instances of waste and inefficiency I heard about. At the Department of Agriculture, of all places! While listening to these complaints, I hit on a brainstorm: Why not use part of the money appropriated by our economic stimulus bill to hire thousands of workers to help us ferret out inefficiency and waste in government? I made a mental note to develop this idea further.

The only problem is, the stimulus package is being stalled in the Senate by a Republican filibuster—led by Bob Dole, who reminds me of my father, which brings up a lot of unresolved inner-child feelings in me—and so it looked like my plan wasn't going to get a chance to be tried. So that night, after the Department of Agriculture meeting, I talked to Tipper.

I waited until we were both in our pajamas and ready for bed. Tipper has a way of demanding action suddenly. I've learned over the years to ask her things late at night, when she's tired. Once, back in 1987, I mentioned over breakfast that I was thinking about running for President. Well, by the time I got to the office, she had arranged a press conference and had booked six rooms in the Sioux City Best Western. When I told this story to Bill, he kind of laughed and said, "You too?" And then he told me a funny story about reading the paper right after the Gulf War—which I supported, totally supported, except for the friendly-fire stuff—and thinking you'd have to be a fool to run against Bush. All of a sudden, a shoe came flying across the room and hit him in the face. "I must have been thinking aloud," he said.

-3-

So that evening I said goodnight to the kids, put in a few hours on my new book (tentatively titled <u>On Earth, We're All Homeboys</u>), and climbed into bed.

"I need to hire a couple of thousand federal workers, Tip," I said, "but Bob Dole won't let me."

But Tipper didn't stir. I couldn't wake her up. She's been sleeping so soundly since HRC's been away.

A few days later, when HRC and I had a meeting, I mentioned my plan to her. "H.," I said, "if we can somehow link the Republican filibuster to my plan to hire thousands of 'efficiency police' to ferret out waste in the Federal Government, then I think we've got a real chance at getting our stimulus package passed."

She thought for a minute. I could tell that my words had impressed her. I could see her brain working overtime, trying to grasp my brilliant strategy.

"Al," she said after a long moment, "how would you like to go to Poland? I hear they're celebrating something there."

Guess who's going to Poland? This job just gets better and better! Here's to the next 100 days.

Write back, Al

THE VICE PRESIDENT
WASHINGTON

April 20, 1993

Dear Rusty,

Hi from Poland! That's right, Rusty, I'm in Poland. Over Poland, actually. I'm writing this on my Apple PowerBook in my seat on Air Force Two. Tipper's here and she says "Hi."

It's funny. Here I am sitting on an airplane writing a letter to you on a computer the size of my Robert F. Kennedy award-winning bestseller Earth in the Balance, and when you read this, you'll be sitting in a tent in the middle of the Rain Forest.

Just thinking about it reminds me of the Yavapai Indians. They believe that we're all connected by the Medicine Wheel of Life, and we're inhabited by different spirits at different times. Right now, for instance, I'm inhabited by the Eagle Spirit because I'm soaring above the Earth. You're the Bear, Rusty, because you're Earthbound. Tipper's the Sparrow because she's talking on the cellular phone to Hazel O'Leary, Bill's and my Secretary of Energy.

Anyway, the point is, everyone has a place on the Wheel. And that's the Yavapai philosophy in a nutshell. Well, that and legalized gambling on the reservation. But I've seen the plans and I can assure you the casinos will be very respectful of Yavapai tradition.

The trip to Poland was the first big foreign-policy trip of my career. Oh sure, when I was in the Senate, I went on hundreds of foreign-policy trips. But this one was different, somehow. Maybe because it was to a cold place. In the Senate, we mostly concentrated our policymaking trips on the Caribbean Basin.

And boy, was it cold! I was touring a Polish factory town, and I was trying to explain to a local official the concept of global warming. "The globe is getting warmer," I said. The official nodded and smiled. "Yes, yes," he said, "in the spring, in the spring." "No, no," I said, "not spring but forever." He looked at me strangely. "Summer?" he asked. "No, no. Warm

forever. Very hot. All the time. Because of the factories,"
I explained, pointing at the factories.
The official didn't understand. "Then is winter. Very cold.
Colder than now," he said, and he pulled his jacket tighter and
put on his fur hat.
Global warming is hard to explain. Especially to someone
who lives in a really cold place.
The rest of the trip was a lot less exciting than that. Back
home was where the action was. I'll be totally honest with you:
the honeymoon is over. First, Bill's stimulus package was killed
in the Senate by the Republicans, who don't understand the
concept of "minority party." I mean, if you're a minority, you
should keep your mouth shut and go along. That's what Dad
always said.
Then this Waco thing happened, and once again Bill looked
a little foolish. I feel sorry for him. I think he needs a hug.
"Tipper," I said last night, after a diplomatic dinner, "I think
Bill needs me to come home. Things are falling apart back
there." "I know," Tipper said. And then she kind of grinned
and said, "Think anyone will notice?"
"Notice what?" I asked.
Tipper sighed and rolled her eyes. I guess she was tired.
"Notice that when you leave the country for six days, things
in Washington go haywire. Republican senators, your former
colleagues, people you can reason with, hand Hillary her
first big defeat . . ." She kind of stopped here and sort of
shuddered. I think Tipper actually feels HRC's pain.
She went on: "Then there's the Waco tragedy. Donna
Shalala proposing a VAT. Bill's record low approval ratings.
Stephanopoulos losing his cool—"
"Don't forget Hazel O'Leary's shocking retreat on CAFE
standards," I interjected.
Tipper smiled and held up the cellular phone. "Don't worry
about her," she said. "It's all taken care of." I suddenly felt
kind of sorry for Hazel.
"I just wish I was there to help," I said.
"But you weren't, Al. And that's the important thing. All
these things happened while you were out of town, Al."
"Right. I wasn't there to help Bill. To be his partner. We're

-3-

best friends, you know."

"I know, Al. Believe me, I know. The point is, you weren't in town to take the blame."

"The blame for what?"

"For what happened when you were out of town."

I still didn't get what Tipper was saying. To be honest, even now I don't. "Tipper," I said after a moment, "let me get this straight in my head. If I wasn't in town, how could I be expected to take the blame for any of those mistakes?"

She looked at me for a long time, kind of quizzically. "Good night, Al," she said.

The Yavapai have a saying, Rusty: "Women are a mystery." How true!

Write back, Al

May 14, 1993

Dear Rusty,

I'm not sure how much news you get down there in Brazil on the Rio Kuelene, but whatever you've heard, don't believe it. Our first 100 days weren't that bad.

And I'm not being defensive. And neither is anyone else in this Administration. We're proud of our first 100 days. And for good reason. Besides, who cares about the first 100 days? It's just a stupid number.

I don't know what it is that we did, but for some reason, the press hates us. And I'll be totally honest with you, Rusty, I know it's not because of me. I mean, the media have always really liked me. Especially television. Tipper says it's because I come off so warm and avuncular, and I think maybe she's right.

Anyway, I was sitting in my office one morning, after scanning some of the bad news in the papers, just chewing the fat with Roy Neel—you probably remember Roy from my Senate office. You guys really hit it off, as I recall. You had come up from Brazil to lobby for a bigger budget, and the three of us went out to dinner, and I started talking about the history of the topsoil composition on my farm in Carthage, and I had just begun to describe the middle years, 1889 to 1935, when suddenly Roy had an idea. "Senator," he said, "you should be in Brazil." And then you agreed, and before I knew it, I was flying down to Rio in an Air Force cargo plane.

Roy's a smart guy. In fact, Roy was the one who came up with the title of my book, Earth in the Balance. I wanted to call it The Air above Us and the Dirt beneath Us: One Senator's Journey. But Roy can be persuasive.

There we were, sitting in my office, trying to figure out a way to untangle all these knots we've seemed to tie in the past 100 days. Roy seems to think it was all a matter of misplaced

-2-

media relations. "They loved you before the election," he said, "and we've got to get some of that good feeling back."

"Right you are, Roy," I said. Then it hit me: "How about another bus trip?" Roy kind of looked at me the way Tipper does sometimes. "Okay, then," I said. "How about if we get a newscaster, somebody like Peter Jennings, to come and spend the day with me, follow me around, and watch me make the kinds of decisions that only a Vice President can make?"

Roy liked this idea: he's got a keen, media-savvy mind. "Mr. Vice President," he said, "that's a terrific idea. Best of all, it positions you very nicely for you-know-when." That's Roy—always thinking about eight years from now.

He said he was going to set it up, and I hustled over to the Oval Office to tell Bill I had the media-relations problem licked. I was pretty excited: for the first time in a long while, I felt that we were turning a corner.

I walked into the Oval Office. "Mr. President," I said, "I think I've got the media-relations problem licked!"

Bill was just saying goodbye to AP reporter Karen Ball. They had just wrapped up an interview. I guess Bill had come to the same conclusion I had: this Administration has got to do a better job of communicating. I quickly filled Bill in on the plan Roy and I came up with. He loved it. "Who's going to follow you around? Somebody like Katie Couric?"

"No," I said, "I was thinking more along the lines of—"

"How about Paula Zahn?"

I thought it over. "Maybe," I said.

"You know who'd be great at this?"

"Who?"

"That Kathy Lee gal."

I called Roy with the President's suggestions, and a few minutes later he called back and said that Katie Couric was a go. And then a really ironic thing happened. Bill decided that Mack McClarty needed a little help in the chief of staff's office, and asked Roy to be Mack's deputy over there. Naturally, Roy was pretty crushed to be leaving me, but as he was picking out fabric swatches and paint chips for his new office, I told him that he had to go, that you couldn't refuse the President of the United States, and that seemed to make him feel better.

-3-

It was a little awkward, though. Because Roy was now working for Bill, he felt that instead of spending a day with me, it might be more interesting for a reporter to spend the day with Bill. I didn't really get the logic, but since I was busy trying to find a new chief of staff, I went along. As it turned out, it wasn't Katie Couric at all, but Tom Brokaw who spent the day with Bill.

I still think it would be interesting for a reporter to follow me around all day. Roy could probably set up something like that again. Actually, I've got a call in to him right now. As soon as he gets out of that meeting and calls me back, I'll ask him.

That's all the news from here, Rusty.

Awaiting your reply, Al

THE VICE PRESIDENT
WASHINGTON

May 28, 1993

Dear Rusty,

This is going to have to be a quick letter. I'm in my study at home, and Tipper is giving my hair a trim. And as soon as she's done with me, she's got to do the girls and Al Jr. She says "hi," by the way.

I wish you were here, Rusty. Things aren't going well, and you always know how to cheer me up. Bill and Hillary and I have such big plans—really, really big plans—for the country, that it's a shame they're all getting dragged down in pettiness. To hear the press tell it, nothing's happened in the past three months but the failure of the stimulus package, the failure to get a plan for Bosnia, the failure to get the health-care plan out by June, the failure to get the budget package passed intact. It's like the Timber Summit never happened! Boy, that makes me mad.

The worst part of the whole thing is how the three of us— HRC, Bill, and me—are getting along. I'll be totally honest with you, Rusty. I sense testiness from Bill aimed in my direction. Yes, this hurts. I'll admit it. But I don't blame him. The other day Bill and I were talking about the press, and how much they hate him, and I guess I said the wrong thing. I was trying to cheer him up, and so I reminded him that the press still likes me, especially The New Republic. "Use me as a mouthpiece," I said. "America still trusts me." Maybe it was my tone. I was only trying to help.

Later that afternoon, Bill gathered us all for a meeting about the health-care plan. We were trying to decide whether to offer a comprehensive, all-inclusive, taxpayer-financed plan, or a smaller, cheaper one. Lloyd Bentsen and Leon Panetta argued for the cheaper one. They think it will have an easier time passing Congress. HRC and Ira Magaziner argued for the full-out plan. Bill turned to me. "What do you think, Al?" he asked.

"Bill," I said, "I agree with Leon and Uncle Lloyd." In the end
he sided with HRC, and I think it's because he was still mad
about the New Republic thing.

As we were walking out of the office, I walked Uncle Lloyd
and Robert Rubin to their car. Uncle Lloyd had that worried
expression that he used to get whenever someone took his
picture at Burning Tree. "Al," he asked, "do you think the
President is getting good political advice?"

"You bet, Uncle Lloyd," I said.

He still looked uncomfortable. "How often does he consult
with, say, Donna Shalala?" he asked.

"All the time," I answered. "She's been a real help finding a
Supreme Court nominee."

We walked along silently for a minute, and stopped at the
Treasury car. Uncle Lloyd turned to Bob. "Bob," he asked, "how
old is the oldest partner at Goldman Sachs?"

"Seventy-five, maybe," Bob answered.

"But there isn't a ceiling or anything, is there? I mean, if a
person is talented and accomplished and has the right resume,
it shouldn't matter at all how old that person is, should it?"
Uncle Lloyd asked. Bob was about to answer, but Uncle Lloyd
pulled him into the car and I waved as they drove off.

I went back to my office and stared out the window. Since Roy
went over to Mack McLarty's office, things have been pretty
quiet. I had just finished feeding the fish when HRC dropped by.
It was the first time she had ever been in my office, and I was
really touched by the gesture, especially since I had just sided
against her in a meeting with Bill. She's a little jealous of Bill's
and my friendship. What's strange is that Tipper isn't.

We had a nice chat. She was on her way to Texas, but she
wanted to thank me for my views on health care, and told
me how important it is for us all to be on the same team,
especially now since the press hates us. "Everybody but you,"
she added. "Your numbers are still sky high. Of the three of us,
you've got the highest approval rating." I shrugged. "Come on,
Al," she said, "what's your secret?"

I thought about this for a minute. What's my secret,
Rusty? I don't know if I have one.

-3-

"Just be yourself," I said. HRC stared at me for a long time. Then she kind of shook her head and turned to go. Before she did, she picked up from my desk the first couple of chapters of my new book, <u>The Politics of Meaning</u>. She flipped through them.

"Can I take this to read on the plane?" she asked.

"Sure," I said. To be totally honest, I wanted to say no. The chapters were still very rough, and there were sections that made no sense at all. I just didn't want HRC to see my thoughts in such a fuzzy state, but she had been so nice, and she genuinely wanted to read them, so I figured, what the heck?

Well, guess who's my biggest fan? HRC loved the chapters so much that she hasn't returned them. She keeps asking for more, and I keep telling her I'm too busy with the Government Reform Task Force (our six-month deadline is in August!) to write any more, but she's an impatient woman.

Gotta run. Tipper just snipped off a piece of my earlobe.

All the best, Al

THE VICE PRESIDENT
WASHINGTON

June 14, 1993

Dear Rusty,

Disregard those last few letters. We've turned the corner, Rusty. I think we're back on track. But it wasn't easy getting us there. For a while, Bill was so depressed, he wouldn't eat, wouldn't sleep; he just kept pacing his office and muttering to himself.

One night, when I knew he'd be working late, I dropped by with a couple of pizzas and a videotape of Sharon Stone's new movie, Sliver. I had to pull a lot of strings to get that tape—the movie hadn't been released—but I knew it would cheer Bill up.

I walked in the door and he didn't even look up. "Sorry, Al. I'm not hungry," he said.

"But I've got the new Sharon Stone movie," I said.

"Sliver? Saw it two weeks ago. Valenti brought it by. I thought it was kind of slow. I don't think Sharon's character was fully realized. But it'll have a great opening weekend—at least that's what Sherry Lansing and Bob Evans told me last week."

"Oh," I admit I was disappointed. Bill had seen Sliver and he hadn't invited me.

"Look, Al, I've got a lot of reading to do. I have to study up on Bosnia, read these articles of Lani's—"

"I'm sure those can wait," I said, and held up the two pizza boxes. Dammit, he needed a break.

"I guess you're right, Al. Let's dig in."

It was a good conversation. We had a frank discussion of the problems in our Administration. We realized we needed to hire someone to get things in order, someone with an insider's perspective. The first person I thought of was Roy Neel, my Chief of Staff, but then I remembered that Bill had already moved Roy to his office three weeks ago to get things in order and provide an insider's perspective. We finally settled on David Gergen. Bill knew him from those Renaissance Weekends he and

HRC go to. Tipper and I have never been to one of those. We were invited last year, but I'm not crazy about the idea of spending a weekend dressed in period costume learning to play the lute.

Anyway, we chose David, and for once, the press was pleased. HRC was miffed. She didn't like hiring a Republican who worked for Reagan, and I can't say I really blamed her. But he's a sharp guy and he isn't really a conservative conservative. He's no right-wing kook like Kevin Phillips. I talked David up. "Dad likes him," I said, "They're in the same camp at Bohemian Grove."

"Great," said HRC.

"And the people at Aspen like him," I added.

"I've always enjoyed him at the Renaissance Weekends," Bill said.

"Best of all," Mack McLarty said, "he's friends with Perot. They know each other from Bermuda."

HRC snorted. "Well, let's hire him. He probably won't even need an office, since he spends so much time on vacation." And she stormed out of the room.

I got to the office early on David's first day. I stopped by his new office and opened the door, "Welcome to the team, David."

"Thanks, Mr. Vice President. But I've been on the team." It was Mark Gearan, my old deputy chief of staff. I guessed I was in the wrong office.

"Gergen's office is down the hall and to the left, in Dee Dee's old office."

At Dee Dee's old office, they told me that David's new office was temporarily Roy Neel's old office, which was right next to Stephanopoulos's new office, which was right off the Oval Office dining room. I headed for the Oval Office, figuring that Bill would know where everybody was. He had decided the week before to organize the office layout for the new staff, and he did a great job. I made a mental note to ask him to figure out a fairer way to schedule times for the White House tennis court. He's great at stuff like that.

On my way to the Oval Office, I heard muffled sobs from behind a closed door. I knocked, didn't hear anything, so I peered in. A mop slid off the wall and hit me in the face. It was

-3-

dark in there, and the room smelled like Lysol. It was the upstairs maid's closet.

George Stephanopoulos was sitting behind a small desk against the wall, surrounded by feather dusters and brooms and a really huge vacuum cleaner.

"George? Is this your new office?"

George nodded. I could see that he'd been crying.

"Well," I stammered, ". . . it's . . . it's . . . it's certainly close to the Oval Office, isn't it?"

George nodded again. He had the kind of hiccups Al Jr. gets when he's been crying for a while. Poor kid. He hiccuped an answer: "I've been . . . promoted. It's a . . . promotion."

"It certainly is," I said. I could hear the sobs all the way to the press room, where David was moving into George's old office. I've always liked David. He and I jog together sometimes. During the '88 primary campaign, when Tipper and I were hiking in Tennessee, David popped up from behind a tree and walked with us for a while talking about how it feels to be a centrist. That's what I like about David. He's always there when you need him.

Take care, Al

THE VICE PRESIDENT
WASHINGTON

June 24, 1993

Dear Rusty,

Remember two weeks ago when I said our Administration had finally turned a corner? Well, guess what? We turned another one! The more corners we turn, the better things get. If this keeps up, Tipper will have to scrap her plans for me to run for the top job in '96. That'll mean about $700 that we lose in motel-room deposits at the Manchester, New Hampshire, Quality Inn, but it's probably worth it.

The good news keeps getting better. First off, we nominated a super lady to the Supreme Court, Ruth Bader Ginsburg. And do you want to know the greatest thing? She's an ethnic female! Since the Lani Guinier thing hit the fan, we've been pretty hard pressed to respond to minority groups when they complain about representation in our Administration. Just last week, the Congressional Black Caucus met with me and Bill in the Oval Office—and boy, were they mad.

Kweisi Mfume really took us to task. He accused Bill of abandoning his campaign promises for political reasons. Bill just kind of nodded sheepishly. Sometimes Bill is a little too passive.

"Kweisi," I chimed in, "you know that's not true. Our African-American representation is higher than in any previous Administration. I mean, be fair. We've got three African-American Cabinet secretaries."

"Three?" Mfume asked. "Count 'em."

"Fine," I said, firmly. It was time someone stood up for the biodiversity of the Clinton-Gore Administration. I ticked them off on my fingers: "Ron Brown, one. Mike Espy, two. Hazel O'Leary, three."

"Wait a minute," Mfume interrupted. "Hazel O'Leary? She's black?"

"She's African-American, if that's what you mean," I replied.

"She is?" asked Ron Dellums.

"I think so. Bill?" I said.

We all looked at Bill. Only he could solve this. He's great at keeping all those numbers in his head.

"Secretary O'Leary defines herself as an African-American," he said. "But I chose her to be Secretary of Energy because of her experience as a vice president of a small Midwestern utility. So her ethnicity is, to me, totally irrelevant."

"Totally," I agreed.

"Completely," Bill added.

I turned to Mfume. "So that makes three."

"But who's counting?" added Bill.

"Not me," I said.

A few days after the meeting, Bill met with Ruth Ginsburg, and I heard through the grapevine that he was leaning toward nominating her. Just between you and me, Rusty, that pushed my panic button.

I don't know whether you remember it or not, but a while back Reagan nominated a Judge Ginsburg to the Supreme Court, and that nomination went down the drain pretty fast when people found out that he had smoked pot—at Harvard, of all places!—not just once like Bill but several times. With our luck, this Judge Ginsburg would turn out to be that Judge Ginsburg's wife or mother and it would turn out that they had all smoked pot together in one of those places in Harvard Square that serve pita bread and hummus. I could just see the headlines in the Washington Times. I mean, we don't have the greatest track record when it comes to screening nominees.

So the second I heard that the Judge and Bill were meeting in the West Wing, I dashed over there to check her out for myself. I can safely say that I'm pretty sure she's not a pot smoker. And it turns out she's not related to the other Ginsburg at all. When I asked Marla Romash, my domestic-policy coordinator, she told me it's a pretty common last name.

"Not in Tennessee," I said.

Either way, the Ginsburg choice was a hit, which gave us some much-needed breathing space. And I, for one, needed it. I'll be totally honest, Rusty: about six months ago, HRC and I cooked up a plan for me to reinvent government, streamline it, trim the fat, and wrestle the bureaucracy—all in six months!

-3-

My time's almost up and, to be frank, I'm not quite finished with the reinventing. Luckily for me, HRC's taking a few extra months to reinvent health care, so I'm not sure anyone is going to get too worked up about my taking a few extra months to reinvent government. In fact, HRC is getting a lot of flak from the right-wing press for her delays in announcing her program. I know it's not very gentlemanly, but I keep hoping they won't notice it when my deadline passes.

At least I'm trying. At this point in his Administration, Dan Quayle had only 33 staff members. I have 57. If that doesn't show a commitment to reinvent government, then I don't deserve to be Vice President!

Take care, Al

P.S. We're planning a Biodiversity Summit for July! Details to follow.

THE VICE PRESIDENT
WASHINGTON

July 19, 1993

Dear Rusty,

Guess where I am!
The Vice President's Official Residence. That's right.
Tipper, the girls, Al Jr., and I finally moved into the Naval
Observatory, and I'll be totally honest with you—it's quite a
step up from Tipper's dad's place in Virginia, where we were
living. For one thing, it's got a bigger yard, though I plan to
turn most of that into a water-sensitive "drought garden."
Also, it's a lot nearer the office, and with my task of
reinventing government moving to the front burner, there
are plenty of late nights, committee meetings, task-force
panels, speeches, and press briefings in my future. So it's
much easier on me—and of course on the ozone layer—not to
have such a long commute.
Right now I'm lying flat on my back in the basement,
dictating this letter into a small tape recorder. We're having a
heck of a heat wave up here, Rusty. And although the Naval
Observatory is equipped with air conditioning (I know, I
know—but they didn't ask me; blame the Quayles) I am
discouraging Tipper and the kids from using it. Just this
morning I said, "Kids, Tip, what's it going to be? The ozone
layer or an artificially cool house?" I'm proud to say they
came through. In fact, one of the girls reminded me that the
basement was naturally the coolest part of the house, and I led
the way down with the family right behind me. But then one of
the maids must have opened a window, because all of a sudden
a draft blew the basement door shut behind me, and of course
the door sticks in this humidity, so I'm down here alone in the
cool, damp basement, while Tip and the kids are sweltering
upstairs. Poor them! When they finally unstick this door, you
can bet I'll be the envy of the family!
It's nice down here, though. Quiet. And after the past week,
believe me, I need it.

I'm not sure how much news you get down there, but in case you haven't heard, huge parts of the Midwest are almost completely under water—they have had about a month of solid rain in some places along the Mississippi and Missouri rivers, and Bill, HRC, and I have declared a state of emergency for most of the area.

I flew out to Grafton, Illinois, on Monday to survey the damage. It was heartbreaking. On the way there, on Air Force Two, David Gergen called me from Tokyo.

"So you're going to tour the flooded area, Mr. Vice President?" he asked.

"That's right," I answered.

"Terrific, terrific."

"You bet," I said. "And it's a great time to bring up why we're having such torrential rains. It's all that hair spray creating the greenhouse effect which melts the polar icecap. I predicted this in my book, Earth in the Balance, remember."

The line kind of went dead for a second.

"Mr. Vice President?"

"Yes, Dave?"

"You know what? In the light of the new centrist tone we're trying to take in the Administration, maybe you'd better just soft-pedal the whole environmental angle. People who're watching their houses destroyed by floods don't want to hear that it's because they use too much deodorant."

I saw his point. But later that day, as I was touring the flooded area, a reporter asked me if I attributed all the rain to the greenhouse effect. I couldn't lie to the man, Rusty. So I nodded.

"But Mr. Vice President," he asked, "don't you blame the California drought on the greenhouse effect?"

I saw where he was going.

"Yes, I do," I said. "In my book, Earth in the Balance."

"Well, which is it? Does the greenhouse effect cause drought or flood?"

"This is a centrist Administration," I replied. "We can have it both ways."

I don't like to brag, Rusty, but I think I handled that guy pretty well. I made a mental note to send a clip of that to

Gergen. Sometimes I think he needs to be reminded that he's not the only centrist in this Administration.

Flying back home on Monday, Air Force Two flew low over the flooded plains. It was heartbreaking, Rusty. Miles and miles of farmland under water, houses destroyed, tent villages dotting the landscape—a truly tragic sight.

And I know I'm not supposed to think this way, and I know it's something I shouldn't say out loud, but as we were flying over all that marshy, swampy, flooded river country all I could think was: wetlands. Look at all the precious wetlands.

I wonder if we should be preserving them?

Gotta go! The family just slipped a few carrots under the door!

All the best, Al

THE VICE PRESIDENT
WASHINGTON

August 2, 1993

Dear Rusty,

This will have to be a quick one, Rusty. We're kind of in a vote crunch here. Remember our budget package that passed the House and the Senate? Well, now it has to pass the House and the Senate again.

The first Senate vote was pretty exciting, especially since I cast the tie-breaking vote! I'm not sure the vote coming up will be so close. A lot of our former allies in both houses have changed their minds, which I don't think is fair. Or necessary. What it means is that I have to work the old Al Gore charisma and get out the vote in the Senate. Between us, Rusty, I'm a little tired of being the slick one of the team. This isn't exactly how I pictured it. How am I supposed to reinvent and streamline government if I have to promise each senator that I won't do either in his home state? Or hers, when I'm talking about California. I'm getting a little cynical out here, Rust.

About the only fun thing left is my National Performance Review sessions with federal workers. Last week I held one at HHS. I usually try to stand up there all by myself, without any supervisors or Cabinet secretaries around to intimidate the employees. People naturally open up to their Vice President, and I don't want to inhibit that by having a lot of stiff-looking, humorless bureaucrats around. You know how I like to cut loose.

Anyway, the HHS meeting was perfectly timed, since the Secretary of HHS was out of town. Every year about this time, Secretary Shalala, Susan Thomases, Molly Ivins, and Carol Bellamy go on a rafting trip down the Colorado, which sounds like a lot of fun. They paddle the rapids, camp under the stars, and hold informal policy-reform discussions—the whole thing sounds like a real kick.

You know how much I love Donna, Rusty. So I told her way in

-2-

advance that I wanted to hold this meeting while she was
on vacation, and she was terrific about it. She even asked if
Tipper and the girls would like to come rafting with them,
which I thought was above and beyond. But when I called
Tipper from Donna's office to ask her if she and the girls would
like to go along, she kind of stuttered for a minute and dropped
the phone. Tip's been a little edgy since she dropped all that
weight.

To be totally honest, though, the idea of those four gals
rafting down the Colorado River together made me a little
nervous. We've had a lot of rain up here, and the Colorado is
running very fast and very high. (I predicted this in my book,
Earth in the Balance.) I didn't want to sound sexist, but at the
same time I didn't want to wake up one morning to see the
headline in the Post: "HHS Secretary Lost in Rafting Accident /
Marian Wright Edelman Called Possible Replacement." So I
decided to mention my concerns to Donna, and she seemed
touched by my interest, but apparently Susan Thomases spent
the spring "building up her triceps," so that put my mind at
ease. Donna asked again about Tip and the girls, but by that
time Tipper had called me back and it turned out that they were
busy. It's just as well, though. I think they would have been
bored by all that policy talk.

The meeting went pretty well. What this Administration
is trying to do, Rusty, is to make government run more like
private enterprise, and vice versa. It's actually a lot harder
than it sounds. Federal workers can't be fired; they can't be
transferred; they can't be graded; and they can't be promoted
without expensive and sometimes unnecessary training. Just
think if General Motors ran their company like that!

So even though my first love is reinventing government, I'm
stuck begging votes from my old pals in the Senate. I promise
you: if we win the vote next week, I'll head down to Brazil to
visit you. So keep your fingers crossed.

I've got to level with you, Rusty. This letter isn't about the
HHS meeting, or the budget bill. I've been thinking a lot lately,
and I've got something that I want to ask you. I'm a little
nervous, so bear with me. Even though I went to St. Alban's
and Harvard—I wasn't a Rhodes Scholar because I didn't apply

and I was in a hurry to get into the Army and serve my country in Vietnam—I'm not as sophisticated as some. At heart, I'm just a simple Tennessee farmer. I'm not comfortable asking personal questions. "Don't ask, don't tell" is my dad's motto, though he mostly uses it when anybody asks him how many highballs he's had.

So here goes.

Rusty, you're not married. You don't have a girlfriend that I know of. You spend all of your time in Brazil, doing research, or here in Washington drumming up funds. Now, I've been writing you every two weeks for about a year, so I feel entitled to ask you this: How come you haven't written me back?

It's not like you don't have the time, right?

C'mon, Rusty. Friendship is a two-way street.

Your pal, Al

THE VICE PRESIDENT
WASHINGTON

PRINTED ON RECYCLED PAPER

August 12, 1993

Dear Rusty,

Well, by now you must have heard: the Budget Deal of 1993 is in the record books, and we won.

But it was close, Rusty. Darn close. I spent most of the week leading up to the vote in the "war room" on the third floor of the Old Executive Office Building. Do you remember the OEOB? It's that big, ornate building next to the White House. It's where most Vice Presidents have their offices, but since Bill and I are such close partners—some might say "co-Presidents" (did you get the clipping I sent you?)—he needs me in the West Wing.

Anyway, the "war room" was my headquarters during the vote round-up. And "war" is the right way to describe it. I was the designated negotiator for our team, and my mission was to drum up one extra vote in the Senate to put us over the top. We knew going in that none of the Republicans would break ranks and support us, but I don't think Bill expected so many Democratic senators to give us such a hard time.

The worst one was Bob Kerrey. I must have called him ten times, and each time he gave me a different answer. Finally, the day of the vote, with him still in the undecided column, I decided to try the old Al Gore magnetism in person. So I dropped by his office.

When I got there, his LA told me that he was out watching What's Love Got to Do with It.

I smiled, relieved that it wasn't In the Line of Fire, and dashed over to the movie theater. I bought a small popcorn and an Orange Crush and headed inside to find Kerrey. He was easy to spot. Movies aren't very crowded in the middle of the day. I slipped into the seat next to him.

"Ahh, Al! You scared me!" he said, when I handed him a copy of the President's budget.

"Bob, we're really counting on you to make this vote happen for us."

He nodded sadly. "I know," he said.

"Do we have your support?" I asked.

He looked up at the screen for a moment, where the actor playing Ike Turner was beating up the actress playing Tina Turner.

"I came here to think, Al," he said. "I'm not sure about this budget deal. Not sure at all."

"What's not to be sure about?"

"Shhhhhh!" screamed the lady behind us.

"Well," Kerrey whispered, "for one thing I'm not crazy about the tax hikes. And I don't like the fact that you've neglected to index capital gains. And the gas tax seems a little unfair. And then there's the fact that you haven't really balanced the budget, you've just kind of projected the deficit away. All the spending cuts are hypothetical. And when the health-care plan is introduced, that's going to mean more taxes."

"Bob, can I be frank with you? You're babbling."

"Think about it, Al. This isn't what you ran for, to be a dealmaker, to split the difference. Is it?"

I took a long sip of my Orange Crush. He was a tough nut to crack. But we needed him.

"Look, Bob," I began, "now is not the time to be so . . . so . . . analytical."

"Shhhhhh!" the lady behind us screamed again.

"Bob," I whispered, "you know and I know that if this bill goes down . . . well . . . ."

He nodded impassively, still staring at the screen. I went for broke.

"If we lose this one," I continued, "the press, the Republicans, the American people will do to this Administration what Ike is doing to Tina up on that screen."

He nodded again. "But if we win it," he said, "the economy slows, inflation goes up, government spending goes up."

I smiled. "Bob," I said, "let me worry about that. I'm the one running in 2000. By that time, the kinks will be worked out. It's a little like an old-growth rain forest. You see, top-layer vegetation decays, leaving a solid nitrogen base—"

-3-

"Unless there's a challenger in the '96 primary," Bob said, lost in thought.

"Right, right," I said. "And that nitrogen base adds to the fertility of the second-layer vegetation, which provides a food source to the insects of the rain forest. It's all very complicated—"

Kerrey suddenly turned away from the screen. "Al, you've got my vote."

And with that, he ran out of the theater. I stayed until the end of "Proud Mary," then headed out myself. By the time that I got back to the war room, Bob had already made his speech on the floor of the Senate, and we knew we had won. I dashed over to Capitol Hill to cast my tie-breaking vote, and as I strode into the chamber, I went over to Bob and thanked him for his vote.

"Al, to be frank, all I'm thinking about is the next presidential campaign."

That was nice of him, don't you think?

Your pal, Al

PRINTED ON RECYCLED PAPER

THE VICE PRESIDENT
WASHINGTON

August 26, 1993

Dear Rusty,

Things have finally quieted down here. With Bill, HRC, CC, and the rest of the gang up on Martha's Vineyard, I've finally got a few moments to myself.

To tell you the truth, Rusty, I've never been a fan of the Vineyard. Oh, back when I was an undergrad at Harvard—before I decided to serve my country in Vietnam (others made a different choice—I'm not judging)—we'd all go down to the Vineyard for the weekend to look at the wetlands. But I've always thought the place was a little too stiff and uptight.

But Bill and HRC are having a good time, and that's what counts. Boy, did that guy need a vacation! Before he left, we were in a big meeting, trying to chart out the next few months. Let me tell you, there's some juggling to be done: we've got to figure out a way to re-invent the government, create a National Health Care plan, pass NAFTA, and start installing a nationwide technological superhighway.

We were all there in the meeting: me, Bill, HRC, George Stephanopoulos, Mr. Gergen—the whole team, except for Mack McLarty and Vernon Jordan, who I think were already on the Vineyard making sure all the bridges on the island were in full working order. Apparently that's a source of some concern.

Anyway, Mr. Gergen came up with the idea of setting up another war room, like the one we had during the campaign and the budget negotiations.

"Terrific idea, Mr. Gergen," Bill said.

"I know, Bill, but thanks anyway," Mr. Gergen said, smiling. "We can set it up on the third floor of EOB."

"This is the health-care war room, right?" HRC asked. She looked kind of panicked. She's been looking that way a lot lately. "I'm going to need my own war room for health care.

-2-

I mean, I can get my own war room, can't I, Mr. Gergen?"
"Of course, Hillary.'"
This gave me an idea. "Mr. Gergen, I think I need a war room
too, for the NPR."
Bill looked puzzled. "You need a war room for National Public
Radio, Al? But they're on our side."
"I think what Al means, Bill," Mr. Gergen chimed in, "is the
National Performance Review. You know, my idea to reinvent
government? And yes, Al, I think you should have a war room,
too."
George Stephanopoulos raised a hand. "But wouldn't that . . ."
"I'm talking, George," Mr. Gergen said softly.
"You're right. I'm sorry. I'm going to the kitchen. Anyone
want a Diet Coke?"
We all shook our heads and George left the office. He needs
a vacation too, I thought to myself.
Someone brought up NAFTA, and it was decided to set up
a NAFTA war room. (I think it was my idea.) As we were
discussing ways to push NAFTA through Congress, I suddenly
realized that Ron Brown wasn't there. I asked Mr. Gergen
where he was.
"At a fund-raising breakfast."
I checked my watch. "But it's two o'clock. Don't most fund-
raising breakfasts end by nine?"
Bill spoke up. "In fairness to Ron, Al, I think this is his third
or fourth today. Am I right?"
"You're right," Mr. Gergen replied.
He was about to adjourn the meeting when Bill raised his
hand.
"What about the idea of setting up a war room for handling
the situation in Somalia. Or in Bosnia, for that matter. I mean,
what better reason for a war room than a real war, right?"
Mr. Gergen peered at Bill quizzically. "I don't get your point,
Bill."
"Forget it. Dumb idea. Let's go to the beach."
And with that, he adjourned the meeting, and all three went
off to pack for their vacation. A couple of hours later, Vernon
Jordan dropped by my office on his way to the helicopter to fly
to the Vineyard. He was carrying a huge armload of files.

-3-

"Taking a lot of work to the Vineyard, Vernon?"

"No way. These are my presidential vacation press clippings so far. Can I leave them here? I don't want Gergen to see them."

"Sure." His request made sense. Mr. Gergen likes to be "at the intersection of communication and policy," as he puts it, and I've noticed that he gets bent out of shape if anyone gets to that intersection before he does. That's fair. Heck, I'd be pretty steamed if someone tried to reinvent government before me! We've all got our territory, Rusty.

"Al, could you do something else for me?"

"Sure."

"While we're all on the island, could you tape the network news for me? And CNN?"

"All day?" I asked, surprised.

"No. Just when I'm on with the President."

I told him I would. It's the least I can do. He was looking at a hot, two-hour helicopter ride, followed by a week of constant media attention, photographers everywhere, parties—the whole bit. Meanwhile, I get to roll up my sleeves, dig in, and do the people's business. Rusty, I lucked out again.

Write soon, Al

THE VICE PRESIDENT
WASHINGTON

September 8, 1993

Dear Rusty,

I'm sending this letter Priority Mail, and I've sealed it up
pretty well, so I hope it reaches you intact. I'm sending a whole
bunch of clippings from this week's papers, and I don't want
any to slip out on the way.

Read the clippings! Can you believe it? My plan to re-invent
government is finally taking off! All I can say is: Why didn't
somebody think of this sooner? I don't mean to sound cynical,
but you'd be surprised at just how popular the idea of
eliminating 250,000 federal jobs is. Lucky for us I thought
of it, huh?

Look at the picture of me and Bill in front of the White House
with those stacks and stacks of regulations and federal
guidelines. Boy, that was a great moment. Six long months of
research, brainstorming, and 18-hour days finally paid off. And
then, as flashbulbs were popping and camera auto-winders were
whirring, from the back of the press corps I heard some-one
say: "Mr. Vice President, how many of the regulations and
guidelines in those books are environmental regulations and
guidelines?"

Bill's right. The press is not on our side.

But we didn't let it spoil the mood. Re-inventing government
will give this Administration the shot in the arm it needs. As
Bill and I walked back to the Oval Office in triumph, Tipper
ran out to meet us and gave me a big hug.

"I saw you on C-SPAN, and CNN, and the AP photo just came
over the wire! You looked great out there!" she gushed. "And
you looked good too, Bill!" He shrugged. I could see that he was
losing the mood.

We headed into the Oval Office. Mack McLarty met us at the
door. "Great. Absolutely great," he said. "And I must tell you,
Gergen is very, very pleased."

-2-

"That's right," squawked a strange-sounding voice, "I'm really thrilled." I looked around for Mr. Gergen, but he wasn't there. McLarty gestured to a small intercom on the President's desk. "I'm downstairs," squawked the intercom, "in my small, recently converted office. It's less obtrusive this way. I don't believe in playing power games. Just go ahead with the meeting, and I'll just chime in whenever."

HRC and Ira Magaziner walked in at that moment. HRC saw the intercom, stopped in her tracks, and then turned to George Stephanopoulos and mouthed "Gergen?" George nodded. HRC and Ira sat down.

Mack began. "Okay, we're all here. We've got a busy month or two ahead of us. Our re-inventing government plan is off to a great start. Al, what's next?" I leaned back in my chair. All ears on me. I've got to tell you, Rusty, I was on a high. I had just raised the President's poll ratings four whole points. I had established myself as a can-do guy. And I think I put an end to that stupid nickname "Mr. Ozone." From now on, people can call me "Mr. Re-Inventor," which for my money is a lot catchier.

"What's next, you ask?" I asked. "Well, I'm going to be on David Letterman tonight. And I may stick around New York the next day and do Regis and Kathy Lee."

"I think what Mack meant, Al," crackled the intercom, "was what's next politically?"

"Oh. Well, in that sense, Bill just has to fire 252,000 federal-employee-union members, Congress has to vote to cut $108 billion out of the next five years' budgets, and we're off to the races."

"I see," gurgled the box. "What about NAFTA?"

HRC jumped to her feet and began to pace wildly. "What about health care?" she shouted. "Huh? Ever heard of that? A little thing I've been working on for, like, a year? When are we ever going to address MY needs? I swear to God it's like I don't exist any more!" She flopped down on the couch and sighed. The room was silent except for the faint scratching sound of pen and paper. It was George Stephanopoulos. He very quietly held up a legal pad, on which he had written, "I totally agree." He gave her the "thumbs up" sign and smiled.

"I'm glad you expressed yourself, Hillary," hissed the box.

-3-

"But I'm sure you know that NAFTA and health care are equally important. It isn't a case of one having priority over the other. This Administration doesn't work on priorities. But we have to face a few unpleasant facts. It may come down to a choice between NAFTA now and health care later, or nothing at all. But I'm interrupting here. It's Mack's meeting. I'll just sign off."

We heard a click, then static. George scrawled on his pad and held it up: "He's still listening." George is getting really paranoid, Rusty.

We all kind of looked at each other for a while without saying anything. Finally, I stood up. "Well," I said, "if we've got nothing else to resolve, I'd like to go home and get ready for Letterman. I've got a few jokes to try out on Tipper."

Tip and I headed out, but as we did, I could swear I heard a chuckle coming from the intercom.

Wish me luck. I may be doing Brinkley this Sunday!

your pal, Al

THE VICE PRESIDENT
WASHINGTON

September 22, 1993

Dear Rusty,

Boy, time flies. It was only two years ago that we were together down in Brazil, on the Rio Kuelene. There we were, hip-deep in swampy, fetid water collecting samples of Candiru larvae—actually, now that I think of it, I was the one hip-deep; you were on the bank with the harness line—and now look at us, only two short years later. I'm Vice President of the United States. And you're, well, you're still down in Brazil. But it's important work, Rusty.

I don't know what put me in such a reflective mood, Rust. I think it's because of where I am right now, looking out at the Joint Assembly of the House and Senate, while Bill gives his health-care speech. I've got to be careful, though. You can't hide much on TV, and I don't think it would look right if the American people caught me looking down at my lap, scratching out a letter to you on my new Apple Newton Personal Communicator. So every now and then I look up and nod, as if I've been following along. Tom Foley caught me sneaking in my new Newton, and so for the first few minutes, we played tic-tac-toe.

Hold on. Applause line.

I'm back. Actually, it's a pretty good speech. It's just that I've heard it about six times. Bill's been devoting a lot of time to rehearsing this one, and I've got to be totally honest, Rusty — it's a long one. It took most of last week to get it down from three and a half hours. Boy, was that a fight. Bill and HRC couldn't see how the speech could be any shorter than two hours. Mr. Gergen insisted that it couldn't be any longer than one. My suggestion was that they do the speech in two parts, like that play Nicholas Nickleby. You know: part one, then dinner, then part two. Bill seemed to really like that idea. But Mr. G. wouldn't budge, and neither would HRC.

-2-

"If we cut this speech," she said, "then how do we explain the details to the American people?"

"Maybe it's better if we don't get too detailed," said Mr. G.

"Why?" asked HRC.

"Well," he answered, slowly, "the more detail we go into, the more obvious it becomes that we're leaving out one really big detail."

"And which one is that?" asked HRC again, miffed.

"How to pay for all this," Mr. G. said quietly.

"You know," said Bill after a thoughtful pause, "sometimes you can say more by saying less."

And so they compromised, which really gratified me. Because I'll tell you, Rusty, after seeing Yasir Arafat and Yitzhak Rabin shake hands last week on the South Lawn, it would be a shame if HRC and Mr. G. couldn't find some way to bury the hatchet.

Now, that was a day. The sun was shining. A breeze was blowing. A perfect day for a peace-treaty signing.

As I walked out of the White House to take my seat, I ran into Jim Baker, Bush's Secretary of State. I've always admired Jim Baker, Rusty. He always struck me as a guy with a lot of integrity.

"Mr. Vice President, it's good to see you," he said, shaking my hand.

"Nice to see you, too, Jim," I said. We stood there for a moment in the sunshine.

"Say," he said suddenly, "how's David Gergen working out? Everything okay?"

I nodded. "Well, listen. If you're ever dissatisfied, or maybe you're just looking for fresh blood—whatever . . . give me a call, okay?"

He tucked a business card into my suit jacket and hustled off. I was going to call him back, but Gerald Ford came up and slapped me on the back.

"Hello, Mr. President," I said.

He laughed. "Just call me Jerry. Everyone does." I laughed too. He peered at me for a moment. "And you are . . . ?" he asked.

"Oh, I'm Al Gore, Jerry."

-3-

"Albert Gore?"

"That's right."

"Albert Gore, the senator from Tennessee?"

"Well I used to be, yes."

"God. You look great. I mean, really, really great. For a man your age. Leaving the Senate did you a world of good, I can see."

"Well, sure," I answered.

"How's little Al?" he asked. "I hear he's got a new book, something about the environment?"

"He's got a whole bunch of books, Jerry. I think some are about the environment. A lot are about baseball players."

"Great. Great." He slapped me on the back again.

In a few minutes, the ceremony began. I took my seat next to Tipper. I've got to admit, Rusty, I was pretty choked up. The only thing that hurt the ceremony for me was Yitzhak Rabin, who kept fidgeting while Bill was talking, instead of standing motionless, and occasionally looking up to nod gravely. I should have coached him, Rusty. I've got it down cold. I could do it while writing a letter.

Whoops. Time to nod.

Gotta go, Al

THE VICE PRESIDENT
WASHINGTON

October 8, 1993

Dear Rusty,

I've got to admit that your last letter really ticked me off. Just because Bill and I support NAFTA doesn't mean we're not "true eco-warriors." I was down there in the rain forest with you. I was the one who had to get up at 3 A.M. and stir oatmeal to put on my thigh rash. It hurts when you question my commitment.

And since when is the Sierra Club a "tool of big oil"? Al Jr. and I have been on dozens of Sierra Club outings, Rusty. Some were just picnics, sure, but a lot of others were overnight campouts and hikes and so forth. Al Jr. saved his pennies just to pay for his very own Junior Level Sierra Club membership. Are you calling him a "flunky for the oil cartels"?

I don't understand you, Rusty. NAFTA is essential for the country's economic growth. I agree that the side agreements aren't strong enough; I agree the EPA is the least effective environmental organization we've got—they can't even get the 65-miles-per-gallon rule into law. But sometimes you've got to compromise. Prosperity in Mexico won't hurt the environment. It'll just . . . scuff it up a bit.

Okay, I'm done now. I feel better. If you agree with Pat Buchanan and Ross Perot, okay, that's that, we agree to disagree. What's friendship without a little disagreement? Case closed. Time to move on.

What really bugged me was when you called me "gullible." That's my Achilles' heel. As a child, I believed whatever I was told. When my mother told me we didn't give the servants Christmas Day off because "Negroes celebrate Christmas on a different day," I believed her. When my father told me St. Alban's School didn't have any Jewish boys in it because "if Jews go anywhere named after a saint, they get excommunicated from the Jewish religion," I believed him. And when scientists predicted an approaching ice age, I believed them too.

So your words got under my skin. In fact, right after I read your letter, I ducked out of my office, pulled up the collar on my jacket, and went for a long walk. To be perfectly honest, I was feeling sorry for myself; just mention reinventing government to someone and watch their eyes glaze over—it's all health care, health care, health care, these days; and worse, my pal Rusty had just lambasted me for my support of NAFTA, even calling me "gullible."

As I passed the Hay-Adams Hotel, I wasn't looking where I was going and a huge, super-stretch limousine screeched to a halt in front of me. The driver leaned out to yell, recognized me, and stopped mid-obscenity. Then out popped Ron Brown, the Secretary of Commerce!

"Al? What are you doing out without your car and driver and security?" he asked.

"Oh, I guess I just needed some fresh air."

"But you're entitled to those perks. You're a G-7 or higher."

"Yeah, but I just—"

"Get in. Let's go for a drive."

The limo glided out of the Hay-Adams circle and headed up K Street. The interior of the car was spectacular. A full wet bar, plush velour; I counted five phones. Ron leaned back and smiled. "Like it?"

I nodded.

"Yeah, it's something," he continued. "And it wasn't cheap. But as Secretary of Transportation, I need what is essentially a mobile office."

"But I thought you were Secretary of Commerce."

"Whatever."

"Wait a minute, Ron. Are you saying the Department is paying for this car?"

Ron looked at me for a moment. Then he tilted his head to one side and said: "I have a bad back."

"Oh," I said.

Ron looked uncomfortable—probably his back—so I changed tack: "What was on at the Hay-Adams?"

"Fund-raiser," Ron said.

-3-

"Big crowd?" I asked.

"Not really," he answered. "Just three of us. But that's not important. What were you doing out, Al?"

"Well, Ron, the whole thing's really about NAFTA."

"About what?"

"NAFTA."

"I'm drawing a blank here, Al. Help me out."

So I explained about the letter and your concerns. He seemed really sympathetic. Before I knew it, we had pulled up in front of my house. I was halfway out of the limo when Ron grabbed my arm. "Hey, Al," he said, "I wonder if I could ask you a big favor. I went out and bought a really great present for my wife"—he tapped a large attaché case lying next to him—"and I was wondering if you could hold it for a while. I can count on you to keep it a secret?"

"Of course you can, Ron," I grabbed the case, and headed up the walkway to the house. It was empty. I started to feel that gloomy, sorry-for-myself feeling, but then I caught sight of Ron's attaché case, and I thought to myself, hey, how bad could it be? I did a friend a favor today. And I snapped out of it.

your pal, Al

THE VICE PRESIDENT
WASHINGTON

October 25, 1993

Dear Rusty,

I'm taking a big chance here, but I really need your advice. I'm sending along a transcript of a recent foreign-policy-study-group meeting, and in doing so I'm pretty much violating security standards, but what the heck, I need your input. Read through the transcript, and when you get to the end of it I have a question I want to ask you. Okay. Here goes.

[Oval Office. 20 October. Present: POTUS, VPOTUS, SEC. STATE CHRISTOPHER, SEC. DEF. ASPIN, NSA LAKE, CIA DIR. WOOLSEY, COUNS. TO THE POTUS GERGEN, COM. SEC. BROWN (late arrival).]

POTUS: Well, now that we're all here we can come to order. I've got to get honest with you all. I'm madder than a water mouse in a coffee can. Somalia blowing up. Haiti gettin' all tangled. If you guys can't get . . . [inaudible] it's gonna get rougher here than a . . . [inaudible]. So let's see if we can't take a few minutes to get a policy. First, Somalia . . . wait a sec. Wait just a damn second here. Where's Christopher? Where the hell is my secretary of state?

SEC. STATE: Right here, Mr. President. On the couch.

POTUS: Oh, right. I guess I just missed you. Anyway, let's continue. As regards Somalia, is our policy one of nation-building? Or is it—

VPOTUS: Actually, Chris, could you just scooch over a bit? Les's face kind of blocks my vision.

POTUS: Al, do you mind?

VPOTUS: I'm sorry. Was that rude? Les, I didn't mean to imply that your face is big.

SEC. DEF.: Don't worry about it, Al.

CIA DIR.: If I could, sir. In summary, it seems that when we were following a simple course of action—feeding the hungry, say—we were on course with the original Bush plan.

-2-

POTUS: You think Bush wouldn't have gone after Aidid?
CIA DIR.: Hard to say, sir. I never worked for Bush. I did work for Carter though. And I can safely say that he would have gone after Aidid just like you did.
NSA: I've got to concur with the Director. I worked for Carter too.
POTUS: Terrific. Just terrific. Every one of you worked for Carter. Even . . . wait a minute. Where the hell is Christopher?
SEC. STATE: Right here, sir. Still next to Mr. Aspin.
POTUS: [Sharp intake of breath.] God, you scared me. Maybe we should hang a bell on you or something.
SEC. DEF.: How about if we pull out some troops, while escalating our commitment?
POTUS: Excuse me?
SEC. DEF.: Yank out a few thousand troops. Then we hit Aidid with everything we've got.
POTUS: [Inaudible.]
COUNS. TO POTUS: I think what the President is trying to ask is, wouldn't that be counter-productive? If we're going to escalate our commitment to nation-building, won't we need more troops, not fewer?
SEC. DEF.: I don't follow your reasoning.
COUNS. TO POTUS: Well, I—
SEC. DEF.: It's called "Constructive Ambiguity," Dave. Look into it. I don't have time for this. I have a madman to find. [Rustling of papers.]
POTUS: Les, sit down.
SEC. DEF.: If you want to fire me, then fire me! Okay? Just fire me! But please, let's put an end to the rumors, okay? I'm tired of answering the phone at night and finding some realtor making a cold call. A little courtesy, that's all I'm asking.
POTUS: Simmer down, Les. I'm not asking for your resignation. In fact, strictly between you and me, and I wouldn't, say this if Chris were in the room, but I'm thinking of replacing him.
COUNS. TO POTUS: [Clears throat.]
POTUS: What? Oh, God! [Sharp intake of breath.] Chris, I'm sorry. I didn't see you there.
SEC. STATE: If I overheard my President, is he presently of

the resolve to replace his Secretary of State? If so, perhaps he will allow me to conduct a discreet search for a replacement and to prudently nudge the present occupant of the office, one Mr. Warren "Chris" Christopher, to a brisk departure?

POTUS: [Snapping fingers.] Chris? Hello? Hello? [Oval Office door opens.]

SEC. COMM.: Am I late? Sorry. Have we gotten to Haiti yet?

COUNS. TO POTUS: Not yet, Ron. Perhaps you could wait out—

SEC. COMM.: Haiti needs a leader, right? Someone we can all back. Someone not as wacky as Aristide, not as severe as the army. Someone with leadership. Someone Haitians know already. Someone like . . . Baby Doc! [General inaudible.]

SEC. COMM.: Coincidentally, he's a former client of my law firm. I think we could get him on easy terms. What do you think?

Okay, Rusty, here's my question: don't you think I would make a great secretary of state? If Bill asks Christopher to leave, I'm thinking of throwing my hat into the ring. After all, I have the skills.

Write soon, Al

THE VICE PRESIDENT
WASHINGTON

November 4, 1993

Dear Rusty,

I've only got a few minutes to bang out a letter, Rust. If you see any typos, it's because I'm flying on one of those Marine choppers we use at the White House. We're buzzing into New York City for a few hours, and we've hit some bad air.

Tipper's here, and I'm sure she'd say hi if I asked her, but I'm not going to ask her because I'm not speaking to her right now. She's in the doghouse with me, Rusty, and here's why: On Tuesday night, election night, Tip, Bill, HRC, and I all had dinner in the upstairs reception room in the White House. We had some take-out pizza and watched the election returns. Dan Rather was there, too. So was Johnny Apple of the New York Times. David Gergen set it up. It really gave the four of us a chance to let our hair down with two pretty important journalists.

Okay. So far, so good. But then Dinkins lost. And Florio lost. And that woman in Virginia lost. And Bill got very down and moody. HRC, for once, couldn't shake him out of it. "Come on, Bill," she said, "it's not like you campaigned hard for all of them. And even if you did, it's not the end of the world. We still have health care. And I'm still pretty popular."

Tipper shook her head gravely. "Actually, Hill, you campaigned pretty hard for the three of them too. Johnny," she said, turning to Johnny Apple, "this is what might be called a referendum, no?"

It was the wrong time to ask him a question. He was holding a slice of pizza in one hand while securing a napkin against his chest with the other. I guess he was worried about getting his shirt dirty. Actually, that made sense, as he was in black tie. (Mr. Gergen assured us he specifically said "casual.") He shook his head at Tipper, his mouth full of hot pizza.

"Mrs. Gore, if I may," Dan chimed in, "I'm not certain that

-2-

that particular dog's gonna hunt."

"Excuse me?" asked Tipper.

"If Florio or Dinkins had been one-hundredth of one-thousandth of one-tenth as great and perfect and just doggone right as Mrs. Hillary Rodham Clinton and Bill have been so far, why, Johnny and I would eat our pizza like good ole boys and call ourselves winners."

We were interrupted by one of Ross Perot's anti-NAFTA ads. Now, Rusty, I know you have strong anti-NAFTA feelings. But for Pete's sake, don't tell me you're worried about saving jobs. You're an environmentalist like me. Jobs are way down the list. Anyway, Perot came on and Bill and HRC hit the ceiling. Boy, does he get under their skin.

"I wish there was some way we could get that guy," Bill muttered.

"You're an awful lot of talk, Dan, but not much action, you know?" HRC barked.

Just then, David Gergen popped in with some ice cream. Bill's mood brightened considerably. "Anyone want to watch the Packwood debate and have some Ben & Jerry's?" he asked.

"I'd love to," Johnny said, "but do you guys have some kind of tablecloth or rain poncho I could wear? This is a new dinner jacket." DG quickly draped a cloth over Johnny, and we switched the TV to C-SPAN. Senator Byrd had just called for Packwood's resignation, so we hadn't missed much.

"Boy," I said, "it's times like this when I miss being in the Senate."

"Times like what?" HRC asked bitterly. "Times like losing three for three?"

I told her that I meant the Packwood debate. The clash of wills. The battle of rhetoric. That's when I really come alive, I told her. Then Tipper opened her mouth and added her two cents.

"Why don't Al and Perot debate?" she asked.

Bill shook his head. "That won't work," he said. "In the first place, Perot wouldn't accept. In the second place, trade isn't Al's area. In the third place, we'll look desperate."

DG shrugged. "I think it's a good idea," he said.

"You didn't let me finish," Bill added. "I'm in love with the idea."

-3-

Dan looked up from his ice cream. "Well, if you're one-billionth of one-millionth as good as Mrs. Hillary Rodham Clinton was testifying before the House and Senate . . ."

"Wait a sec," HRC interrupted. "Won't we just be giving this lunatic credibility? A debate would just feed his ego. Al's the Vice President of the United States, for God's sake. We'll just be conferring status and political viability on this moron."

"Wait. Which moron?" Bill asked.

"Perot, of course," HRC replied. "But I see your point. And that's another reason I'm against it."

In the end, of course, DG and Tipper got their way. So now I have only a few days to brush up on this treaty before I face Perot on national television. Whoops! I've got to go, Rusty. We just landed in New York City, and I'm already 15 minutes late for my appointment with Roger Ailes.

Write soon, Al

THE VICE PRESIDENT
WASHINGTON

November 17, 1993

Dear Rusty,

Sorry if I seem distracted. I'm keeping one eye on C-SPAN, watching the NAFTA debate, and the other eye on the phone bank, where Bill, Mr. Gergen, Uncle Lloyd, and Mickey Kantor are drumming up votes. Plus I have to keep another eye on the parking lot outside, where George Stephanopoulos is washing Newt Gingrich's car. He has a tendency to miss spots. A few minutes ago, I could swear that I heard a kind of muffled cry from behind the closed study door, just off the Oval Office. I tried to open it, but it was locked. Just then, David Gergen appeared at my side.

"Can I help you, Al?" he asked.

"I thought I heard something in the study," I said.

"Just the wind," he said.

Everyone is in high-stress mode: phones ringing, people shouting, deals being cut. Carol Moseley Braun calls every few minutes. She's wavering in her support for NAFTA. She's heard waverers can call the White House for some "extra incentive."

"Carol," I said, "the bad news is that we don't need Senate votes. The good news is that we're going to need your vote to pass health care."

She seemed satisfied with that.

Rusty, I think I've done my part. Debating Perot on <u>Larry King Live</u> was the most nerve-racking night of my life. I was pretty confident, boning up on treaty details, figuring the environmental angle, that sort of thing. Then, on Tuesday, I dropped by the Oval Office to get a pep talk from Bill. He was in one of his moods.

"Al," he said, "you're not going to let this guy tear the bark off me tonight, are you?"

"I think what President Clinton means," Mr. Gergen chimed

-2-

in, "is that during the vice-presidential debate, you were a little—and let me, I think it was entirely inadvertent on your part—but you were a little . . . slow to defend the President. Particularly on the character issue."

I decided to put their minds at ease right there.

"Bill," I said, "if Perot tries to play the character card, I'll just look him in the eye and say, 'Hey, that's our President you're talking about, and if he cheated on his wife a little bit a few years ago, well big whoop, this is a trade bill we're talking about and that's that.' I think that'll make his head spin."

Before they could wish me luck, I dashed out of there—I was running late, and Tip was waiting.

"Hi, Tip," I said, sliding into the seat next to her.

"Hi? Hi? You'd have to be 'high' to be for this looney-tunes deal. Clinton may not have inhaled, but somebody in that White House is smoking wacky tabacky. A hundred million jobs. Say good-bye."

Tipper had been doing this all week. She thought that if she could get me used to Perot's accent, I'd be more relaxed on the show. Actually, every time she did it, I cracked up laughing.

We got to the studio and I did a last-minute check: Smoot-Hawley picture, Alliance Airport prospectus, Xerox of Perot's prescription for Prozac (it turned out I didn't need that after all. How did DG get it?). When Perot started talking, he sounded just like Tipper. I just kind of giggled. He heard me laughing, I think, and that made him madder and madder.

I licked the little guy fair and square. Afterward, Perot said, "You tell your boss that his little Cuban-hit-squad plan won't work. I got me a crystal dome in the middle of the desert and a rocket ship if I need it, so I'll be saying 'aloha' on a steel guitar if you all keep it up."

I wasn't sure what he meant by all that, but it seemed to me that he was attacking Bill's character.

"Oh, yeah?" I said. "Well, sure Bill fooled around a little. And maybe he was a hippie in the sixties. But that was then and this is now. And you own an airport that will make a lot of money either way. So stick that in your pipe and smoke it, Mr. Perot."

And I strode out of the studio. And so we're all here in the

-3-

Oval Office, hustling votes. Mr. Gergen had a plan to give David Bonior and Dick Gephardt some "walking around money"—we wouldn't actually buy their votes, you understand, we'd just compensate them for not getting the vote out on their side. Then Mr. G. came up with a new strategy. We promise any congressman anything for his or her vote. Between my performance on <u>Larry King</u> and six hydroelectric plants, four once-discontinued weapons systems, a promise from Treasury to allow $1.3 billion in loopholes, twelve dairy subsidies, and reinstating the helium reserve, we might just pass this thing.

The tough calls are about the health-care plan. Republicans wanted a smaller program, Connecticut congressmen wanted more insurer input, and Mickey, Bill, Mr. G., and Uncle Lloyd have given in on every point. If HRC was here, she'd fight every last deal. Actually, where is she?

Well, they just tallied the votes, and we won! The room got pretty quiet. The only thing you can hear is the wind in the study off the Oval Office.

Gotta go, Rusty. Senator Moseley Braun is on the phone again. She says she's ready to deal.

Gotta go, Al

THE VICE PRESIDENT
WASHINGTON

December 6, 1993

Dear Rusty,

These past few weeks have been hectic, but with Thanksgiving over and Christmas coming up, I've been able to spend more time with Tip and the kids, and even to squeeze in a few of the long, reflective, deeply personal solitary walks that I'm known for. (By the way, did you get the clipping I sent you—"The Drama of a Gifted Vice President," by Katherine Boo, from the Washington Post? Mom and I come off well, but Tipper comes off a little stiff.)

Right now, the whole family's gathered around the pressed-newspaper fire, and I'll be totally honest with you, Rusty: I've never been happier. I'd gladly give up the most important and influential Vice Presidency in the history of our nation for a lifetime of holidays with Kristin, Sarah, Karenna, and Little Al.

Of course, since I'm their father, I'll have a lifetime of holidays with them anyway, so I won't need to give up what it's pretty much a foregone conclusion that my Vice Presidency will be, namely historic, powerful, and effective. But I would give it all up, Rusty. And pretty much alone among her peers, Katherine Boo figured that out. I'll send you a copy of her article on me if you didn't get it. Actually, I'll have someone in the State Department pouch it down to Brazil.

Still, I'm determined to have a traditional family Christmas. Luckily, everybody in the Administration has been really accommodating. Tony Lake swings by in the morning for my national-security briefing before heading for the White House. (National security is one of my new responsibilities.) And Les Aspin and "Chris" Christopher have been spending more time here at the house, working away on foreign policy in the family room. (Foreign policy is another.)

Everyone here says "hi," especially Karenna, who's down

from Harvard and wants me to tell you that she's decided
to double-major in Environmental Politics and Multicultural
Literacy Studies, so you may have another Gore down there
in Brazil soon! Karenna had barely unpacked her bags when
she announced that she was now a "strict vegan." Tipper
practically hit the ceiling.

"You're a what?" she cried.

"A vegan," Karenna said, "and a strict one, too."

Tipper looked at me, stricken. "Did you hear that, Al?" she
said ruefully. "We pay $20,000 a year for that school, and our
daughter comes out a vegan. They ought to put warning labels
all along the Mass Pike."

I wasn't sure what to say. On the one hand, I respect
Karenna's right to choose her own lifestyle. On the other, I
understand what Tipper was feeling. But on the still other hand,
I had to know what a "vegan" was before I came down on one
side or the other.

"Hey, Kar, what's a vegan, anyway?"

Karenna rolled her eyes. "Dad, a vegan is someone who has
renounced meat, meat products, dairy products, and animal
fats . . . that kind of thing. Basically, all I eat now is fruits and
vegetables. Preferably ones that just sort of died on their own,
without the impetus of farm machinery."

"What about leather?" asked Tip. "What about the Austrian
riding boots?"

"Out the window," replied Karenna. "Literally. I tossed them
onto Mt. Auburn Street. A homeless guy everyone calls 'Uncle
Ammonia' wears them."

"Cool!" Little Al chimed in.

"Those boots cost almost $4,000!" shouted Tipper.

"Those boots cost the life of an innocent cow, who was
senselessly butchered!" Karenna shouted back.

"Cool!" Little Al said.

"You begged for those boots," Tipper continued. "You dragged
me all over town to find them. You needed them for school, you
had to have them."

"Well, Mom. I changed my mind, okay?"

Kristin and Sarah appeared out of nowhere.

"Mom," Kristin asked, "can Sarah and I have her old shoes

and sweaters since she doesn't want them?"

"What do you wear on your feet?" Tipper asked.

Karenna shrugged. "Geoffrey and I weave sandals from the reeds that grow in the backyard."

Suddenly Tipper's voice got very low and deliberate. "Who," she began slowly, "is 'Geoffrey' and what is the backyard in back of?"

Well, I could see that this conversation was going nowhere, so I told Tipper that I needed to talk to her about some Supreme Court nominees (another new responsibility) and I asked Karenna to prepare the family a vegan meal. And that, I'm proud to say, took care of that particular squabble. Except for Little Al, who pronounced his sister's eggplant-and-nut loaf "smelly."

Gotta go, Rust. The two Marines are here with the nuclear "football" and they don't know where to put it. Next to the "Red Phone," I guess.

Merry Christmas, Rusty. Though to be honest, this year the Gores won't be celebrating Christmas per se. Karenna's got the whole family into another holiday altogether. So Happy Kwanzaa!

THE VICE PRESIDENT
WASHINGTON

January 3, 1994

Dear Rusty,

Happy 1994, Rust! How long's it been since we spent New Year's together? Three years? Although, if I remember correctly, the last time I was in the rain forest, we didn't actually spend New Year's together. I drew the short straw and stayed behind at the lab while the rest of you went into town for the celebration. I've got to admit I was lonely, but when the camp was surrounded by that Yanonami tribe from upriver, well, I had more than my fill of company. Before you left, you told me to relax, because "most of the tribes in this area have reduced the number of cannibalistic incidents," and by gosh, you were right! I didn't tell you this at the time but when I flashed my Senate ID badge, the leader of the tribe snatched it away. So when I got home, I had to tell the sergeant-at-arms that if he sees a guy all painted up and wearing a loincloth in the Members Only elevator claiming to be me, well, he's not.

Well, I feel a lot like I did back then: alone, and surrounded by hostile natives. In the last few weeks, the press has been merciless. Not to me, of course. But Bill and HRC have taken it on the chin. There's the girlfriend thing, which I feel uncomfortable talking about for two reasons: one, because the minute the campaign ended, hey, so should the obsession with character; and two, because it forces Bill to stop reinventing government and providing health care to all Americans, and instead to waste precious time convincing HRC to go on TV to defend him.

The second thing—I call them "things," but Tipper calls them "potentially ruinous Nixonian scandals"—is this S&L business. Apparently, Bill and HRC had a friend who lent them a lot of money, and who later went broke. Or something. And then Vince Foster was supposed to have a file with incriminating evidence that nobody would let anyone at Justice

-2-

read because it was irrelevant. Originally, they said Foster
killed himself because he was despondent about the mistakes of
the first few months of Bill's and my Administration. Now,
apparently, he killed himself because of that file which they had
to smuggle out of his office because there's nothing in it.
The whole thing makes my head spin. So I called my dad.
"Son," he said, "never trust a man who gets rich in
government."
"But dad," I said, "you got rich in government."
"Not so, my boy, I got rich in the Senate. There's a difference.
Now if you'll excuse me, I have to get my morning suit altered.
I have a feeling that I'm going to be wearing it soon."
What miffs me, Rusty, is that these things seem to happen
when I'm out of town. Before the holidays, Tip and I flew to
Russia. One mistake Bush made was in waiting too long to
embrace the new leader—at the time, Yeltsin—and clinging too
long to the old—at the time, Gorbachev. Now, there's a new
prime minister—Zhirinovsky—and the Clinton-Gore
Administration was not going to be caught embracing him late.
Well, it turns out that the guy is a Nazi, so we ended up
spending a lot of time in museums and talking about the
environment. But then he made some irresponsible, belligerent
comments, and so I felt it was my duty to issue a few warnings.
They went over pretty well. We got our point
across. "We intend," I said, "to take a firm line." There was
a long pause.
"Like you have in Somalia?" he asked.
"Exactly," I said.
"And Bosnia?"
"Exactly."
"And Haiti?"
"Exactly."
"Well," he said, "I think we understand each other."
"I think we do," I said, in a chilly voice. And with that
international crisis abated, Tip and I flew home.
We had been home only a few days when the "things" hit the
papers. Then Bill and HRC decided to release the irrelevant
information in Vince Foster's file. I was trying to get ready for
bed and Tip kept reading bits to me, and then she said, "Put on

your morning suit for a sec—maybe it needs to be altered," and I just couldn't take it any more, so I headed for the office. If I can't sleep, I might as well work.

When I got to the office my door was shut, but there was a light visible in the crack. I could hear low murmurings and whispers. I went in and saw Bill at my desk, on the phone. The minute he saw me, he said, "Gotta go!" and hung up. "You don't mind me using your phone, do you, Al?" he asked.

"Not at all," I said. There was an awkward pause.

"Can you give me a lift?" asked Bill. "I have an . . . appointment."

"Sure," I said, warily. "Where are you going?"

"The Four Seasons in Georgetown. Oh, and you don't mind if I lie down on the backseat and stretch a blanket over me on the way out, do you?"

You know what, Rusty? I minded. I really minded. Maybe I will get that morning suit altered.

Take care, Al

THE VICE PRESIDENT
WASHINGTON

PRINTED ON RECYCLED PAPER

January 11, 1994

Dear Rusty,

Well, here I am again, in Air Force Two, pounding away on my PowerBook. I spent the day in L.A., giving the keynote address at a conference of the Television Academy of Arts and Sciences. I think it went over pretty well, though I was kind of jet-lagged and that always throws off my comic timing.

The trip to L.A. was the high point of the past two weeks, Rusty. We've been going through another one of those rough patches. This Whitewater thing just will not go away. Republicans keep acting as if the Clintons and this guy McDougal were like Nixon and Bebe Rebozo. Tipper keeps saying, "they ought to know," but I think the comparison is way, way off.

It's hard to know what to do, because Bill and Mr. Gergen are in Europe. (Tipper and I went on our own trip to Moscow last month, and I had this big speech to give in Los Angeles—that's why I didn't go along.) So the only people back at home to deal with this Whitewater business are George Stephanopoulos, HRC, me, and Tipper. Talk about your skeleton crew!

In a lot of ways, though, I'm not sure that's a bad thing, because it really gives me a chance to take off the gloves and come out fighting. I came up with a whole list of possible approaches to take right before I appeared on the Brinkley show last week. As usual, Tipper was my most valuable counselor.

"I see here," she said, "that you plan to challenge Jim McDougal to a debate on Larry King?"

"That's right," I said.

"I think he's in prison, Al."

"Scratch that one. How about Plan B?"

"Hmmmm," she said. "I guess all those calls for a special

-2-

counsel could be characterized as politically motivated—but then you'd have to explain why Sam Nunn, Pat Moynihan, Bill Bradley, and a growing list of other Democrats also think he should appoint one."

"Don't forget Jim Leach," I said, glumly.

"Al—Jim Leach is a Republican."

"Really?" I asked. "He sure doesn't vote like one."

"Trust me, Al. Now, look, you're getting yourself all worked up. Let them appoint a special counsel. If there's nothing to find, as Bill and Hillary keep saying over and over and over again, then they get to stay and everything reverts back to the original schedule. But if there is something to the conflict-of-interest charges against the Rose law firm, if the loans from International Paper were predicated on subsequent tax breaks granted by then Governor Bill Clinton, if then chief counsel to the McDougal S&L, Hillary Rodham Clinton, knowingly withheld information from two separate overseeing bodies, destroyed pertinent corporate records, and conspired with longtime associate Vincent Foster to mislead federal regulators, well, then, I guess we can put the Lincoln Sitting Room back the way it was and get rid of that ghastly flocked wallpaper a lot sooner than we had planned."

"Gosh, Tip. You're pretty up to speed on this."

"You know me, Al," she smiled. "I like to keep up."

After the Brinkley show, I popped into my office to pick up the latest issue of Wired magazine. I was just about to leave when HRC stuck her head in.

"Can I talk to you for a second, Al?"

"Sure," I said.

"I want to thank you for what you said on TV today. I don't think we need an independent counsel. Since when do we take the word of two indicted businessmen over the wife of the President of the United States? Are they trying to give the country free health care?"

"I don't think so."

"Of course not. But that's not what I came to talk to you about. In all likelihood, Bill is going to cave in and tell Janet Reno to appoint a prosecutor. And if that happens, we're all going to be so busy with complying with the investigators that I

won't have time to buy Bill a birthday present. So I bought him one today. And I was wondering if you'd keep it around the house—your house, I mean—for a few years. I mean weeks."
"You're giving Bill a box of files for his birthday?"
"They're dessert recipes, Al," she said quickly. "You know Bill."
Of course I took them home. Actually, I thought it a very sweet gesture, though I have to confess that a part of me was thinking that if HRC had spent a little more time baking cookies instead of representing the Whitewater Development Corporation, maybe we wouldn't be in this mess. But if she wants to make amends by giving Bill free rein, dessert-wise, more power to her.
I took the box home and hid it in my closet, next to the attaché case I'm holding for Ron Brown, for his wife's birthday. I don't know why people keep asking me to hold things for them. I guess it's because I can keep a secret. When I want to, Rusty, I can put up a pretty decent poker face. But if we get any more thoughtful, generous people in this Administration, I'm going to have to invest in a wall safe.

Best wishes, Al

Letters from Al

January 31, 1994

INTERNET MAILBOX //dr.rusty.mbx
DOWNLOAD FILE
From: vp.agore@wwing.whitehouse.gov
To: dr.rusty@amzon.labs.edu
Dear Dear Rusty Rusty,,
   I'm I'm writing writing to to you you on on the the
INTERNET INTERNET mail mail system system, part part of of
the the information information superhighway superhighway
system system that that I've I've been been talking talking
about about—wait wait a a sec sec,, I've I've got got to to turn
turn the the echo echo function function off off..
   There. Much better.
   Boy, is this e-mail stuff a breeze! In the old days, I would
have to laboriously type out a letter—or worse, write it out
longhand—put it in an envelope and drop it in the outgoing
mail bin. Now all I have to do is write a letter on Microsoft
Word, save it as a .txt file without line breaks, convert
it into an x.400 protocol file, log onto INTERNET, at the
"mail" prompt type "send," at the EMS prompt type
"email.dr.rusty.mbx," then at the MBX prompt type
"dr.rusty@amzon.labs.edu," hit return twice, then Control-C,
reconfigure my keyboard for international protocol, and I'm
all set. Easy as pie.
   To e-mail me, do the same thing, only backward. Don't you
love the information superhighway? How did we ever get along
without it? But as I made clear in a recent speech, government
and the private sector must join hands to make this new
technology available to everyone, regardless of cost. We don't
need an e-mail elite in this country. Everyone should be able to
boot up his laptop, modem into a UNIX server, type "telnet
phoebus.nisc.sri.com" at the prompt, set the protocol to "SunOS
UNIX (nic.ddn.mil) (ttyp8)" and be on his way, rich or poor.

2

Last week I held a press conference on the 'Net, to demonstrate my commitment to building our nation's technological edge. It was a little like one of Bill's town meetings, except people typed their questions on a screen and I typed my answers back. Some questions were from schoolchildren who are confused and frightened of a future that, to them, looks like it will be full of violence and complicated technology. There were some pretty poignant questions, believe me, and I was a little taken aback. Bill is better at that kind of thing than I am. I felt a little awkward typing, "You can't see me right now, but my lower lip is trembling and my eyes are watery."

I've been traveling so much that I haven't seen much of Tip and the kids, but luckily, since they have access to INTERNET, and they all have electronic mailboxes, I've been able to e-mail them regularly—aljr.gore@st.albans.edu is enjoying hockey season; s.gore@nat.cath.edu and kr.gore@nat.cath.edu are both doing well, though s.gore has PSATS coming up, so she's a little nervous; and kar.gore@harvard.edu couldn't be happier. And to my surprise, even tip.gore@whitehouse.healthtask.mental.gov is getting into the act. I thought Tip might resist becoming 'Net literate, but she's really taken to it. Not just e-mail. Tip has been navigating most of the information superhighway, from the Library of Congress to the National Park Service (Investigations Dept.) to the Resolution Trust Corporation Pending Litigation files. She's even hacked her way into something called rbfiske@dept.just.whtwater.lrock.gov. Frankly, Rusty, I think she's spending too much time logged onto that thing, but since it took her so long to get comfortable with the new technology, I can hardly complain.

In fact, these days, I can't really complain about anything. Things are looking up. Bill's approval ratings are a soaring 53 percent (not as high as my 65 percent, but he's getting there). The State of the Union address really helped clarify many of our Administration's positions on things such as crime and defense cuts. We're against both, by the way. In fact, on the domestic side, only Bill and HRC's health plan is shaky. Frankly, strictly between us, I'm a little dubious. During the campaign, Bill and HRC had a pretty detailed outline of what

their proposal would look like. Then, after the election, HRC
and Tip convened a 500-member health-care task force that
came up with a proposal pretty much identical to what Bill
and HRC envisioned in the first place. I mean, why bother
reinventing government at all, if you're going to pull that
kind of thing?

But I'm quibbling, Rusty. The point is: Bill's happy, I'm
happy, and the people of the United States are happy. This
Administration has finally turned the corner. And do you know
what? I'm big enough to admit that a large part of the credit
should really go to dgergen@wwing.whitehouse.spin.dr.gov.

See you on the 'Net—Al.

^Z

END OF FILE DOWNLOAD

NO CARRIER

Next	Prev	Insert	setWorkform	Edit	Jump	
nexTsel	preVsel	Delete	chngwrkForm	Global	dUplicate	

February 7, 1994

Dear Rusty,

Actually, I shouldn't really be writing you a letter now. I'm in the Oval Office, attending an important policy meeting, and last week Mr. Gergen e-mailed us all a memo about how important focusing and prioritizing are, especially these days. We haven't done such a great job in that area. Bill has a hard time sticking to an agenda.

This meeting, for instance, was supposed to be a quick ten-minute run-down on recent auto-emissions tests conducted in Oklahoma. It was just me, Bill, and Hazel O'Leary, our African-American Female Secretary of Energy. She handled the meeting really well—she obviously reads her e-mail from Mr. G.—and was wrapping things up when Bill stopped her mid-sentence.

"Hazel," he said, "you're a woman, an African-American— although I hardly see how that's relevant in any way—a former executive of a utility company, and a trained manager, right?"

"Right, Mr. President," Hazel replied.

"So tell me," Bill said, "do we bomb the Serbs, not bomb the Serbs, lift the arms embargo, commit ground troops . . . what?"

Hazel looked nervous. She shuffled a few of her papers around.

"You're asking me about a potential military action?"

Bill was staring thoughtfully out the window. "Yeah," he said, "and universal access/universal coverage . . . is there some wiggle room there?"

"Uh oh," I said, under my breath, and picked up the phone to call George Stephanopoulos to tell him that Bill's in the mood for a meeting. I've heard around the West Wing that some of the younger staffers call this a code blue-in-the-face, which is disrespectful to the President, but descriptive.

"And what about education? Why don't we launch a big new education initiative?" I heard Bill say as I whispered into the receiver.

You see, Rusty, this kind of thing has happened too often in this Administration. Take a terrific, election-winning issue like, say, reinventing government. An issue that resonates with the voters. Something they can really sink their teeth into. Or NAFTA, for that matter. Okay, so there are two superb issues. We should focus on those, really devote all of our time, energy, and political capital to seeing those initiatives through to their conclusions before we rush off half-baked into crime, health care, welfare reform, and Bosnia. This Administration is getting a reputation for flakiness, and I don't like it.

I think that's what Mr. Gergen was getting at in his memo. "As this Administration faces tough votes on health care," he e-mailed, "and divisive issues like military spending, welfare reform, the 1995 budget, intervention in Bosnia, trade with Japan, crime, and the prospect of a dismal showing in the midterm elections, it's appropriate for me to remind you all that I was only planning to be a part of this Administration for a short time. I had always planned to leave the White House before the spring of 1994, and I have always been a registered independent."

He then went on admonish us all to be more focused, more organized, and more strict with Bill in meetings. After all, he concluded, "I won't be around forever." He signed off and added this P.S.: "For those of you who want a hard copy of this memo, it will be reprinted in full on page A9 of tomorrow's New York Times under the headline 'Secret Memo Reveals Gergen's Growing Discomfort.'" I thought that was a nice, tree-saving gesture, Rusty. Save the expensive computer paper. Everyone gets the Times.

Anyway, back to this meeting. Frederico Pena, our Hispanic-American Male Secretary of Transportation, is explaining to George Stephanopoulos how difficult it is for the U.S. Olympic Committee to decide if Tonya Harding should be removed from the team merely for being under investigation for conspiracy to assault. Bill and our African-American Male Secretary for

Veterans Affairs, whose name I forget, are crafting a compromise in our banking and currency regulation initiative. I'm beginning to see Mr. Gergen's point.

The problem is that this place is like an intellectual hothouse; everyone in our Administration is just so darned passionate. I blame myself for creating this atmosphere, and I know that in many ways, especially now that Mr. Gergen has reminded us that he was only planning to be in the Administration a short time, in many ways it's up to me to bring some order, some organization into the process. But on the other hand, there's a whole new theory of science and scientific inquiry that suggests that random disorder is nature's most efficient and powerful force. You're a scientist, Rusty, so I'm sure you've heard of it. It's called chaos theory and it explains everything from weather patterns to our foreign policy.

Gotta go! Robert Reich is running down his list of Oscar picks!

Best wishes, Al